Praise for the Innovative Leadership Workbook for Global Leaders

In today's global economy, it is critical that successful leaders develop strong leadership skills. Leaders need a solid grasp on the key skills required to operate anywhere and, without effective skills, leading across borders can result in frustration and a sense of personal and professional failure. This timely and efficient workbook delineates core competencies and provides a roadmap to guide leadership development.

Kelechi A. Kalu, Ph.D., Associate Provost for Global Strategies and International Affairs; Professor, African-American and African Studies, Office of International Affairs, The Ohio State University

■■■■■■

Strong leaders need a combination of strong business acumen and cultural awareness, and this workbook is just the resource to help a leader develop them. The case study illuminates the challenges a successful global leader faces as he navigates his own development. The insight into his process is invaluable for you to build upon your leadership success.

Doug Wong, Vice President, Nanpao Coatings, Asia

■■■■■■

Our experience and training as global leaders tends to focus our attention outward on the cultural contexts within which we do business. Wisdom shows the importance of the inward development of how we make sense of the complexities we face and our resilience in facing turbulent environments. This workbook weaves together both with very practical, time-proven processes, highlighted with great examples from colleagues in the global trenches.

Jim Ritchie-Dunham, Ph.D., President, Vibrancy Global, Adjunct Faculty at EGADE Business School (Mexico), Harvard, MIM Thunderbird School of Global Management, MBA ESADE (Barcelona)

■■■■■■

The *Innovative Leadership Workbook for Global Leaders* provides existing and aspiring leaders with a compelling step-by-step approach to increase their leadership effectiveness and impact.

Marc Grainger, Head of Human Capital Management, Credit Suisse

■■■■■■

Innovation and global leadership are the pillars of the 21st century workplace. More than ever this era demands that competent, innovative, and adaptable people lead organizations. This workbook provides managers and other leaders with the necessary strategies for personal growth and development.

Natasha Pongonis, Co-Founder at Nativa and CEO at OYE! Business Intelligence

Leading globally is a challenging role that requires unique skills and competencies. The three authors of this workbook share their extensive research and vast experiences as they carefully guide the reader on the path to becoming an innovative global leader. This is a great book!

Michael Marquardt, Professor, Elliott School of International Affairs, George Washington University, Author of Leading with Questions

■■■■■■

Great leaders are lifelong learners. The concepts in this workbook provide a framework and give examples to support your global leadership skills development through a series of clearly defined exercises and reflection questions. This proven process will guide your learning and build on your success.

Satya Nand, Business Manager – Middle East, Coil & Extrusion Coatings, International Paint Saudi Arabia, Ltd.

■■■■■■

The *Innovative Workbook for Global Leaders* is an indispensable tool for those individuals who want to excel in the global marketplace. Harvard Professor Rosabeth Moss Kanter has observed that those who want to participate in our changing world must embrace "world class concepts, connections, and competence." The thoughtful approach offered in this unique workbook provides valuable guidance to those seeking to fully embrace world class as they seek to become meaningful and successful global leaders.

Gregory S. Lashutka, Former Mayor, City of Columbus, Past President, National League of Cities

■■■■■■

As our businesses and universities globalize, leaders need strong technical skills and also strong global leadership skills. The most successful leaders best augment their technical skills with self-awareness, authenticity, an ability to manage multiple highly complex issues, and an ability to navigate organizational politics with finesse. This workbook helps strong performers build on those skills to become either stronger individual contributors or highly effective global leaders.

Ahmet Selamet, Ph.D., Chair, Department of Mechanical and Aerospace Engineering, The Ohio State University

INNOVATIVE LEADERSHIP WORKBOOK

FOR GLOBAL LEADERS

Field-Tested Processes and Worksheets for Innovating Leadership
and Creating Thriving Organizations

MAUREEN METCALF

STEVE TERRELL, EDD   BEN MITCHELL

FORWARD BY WILLIAM BRUSTEIN,
VICE PROVOST FOR GLOBAL STRATEGIES & INTERNATIONAL AFFAIRS, THE OHIO STATE UNIVERSITY

First Published by
Integral Publishers
1418 N. Jefferson Ave.
Tucson, AZ 85712

Published in the United States with printing and
distribution in the United Kingdom, Australia, and
the European Union.

ISBN: 978-0-9896827-3-2

First Printing March 2014

Cover Design, Graphics and Layout by
Creative Spot - www.creativespot.com

Acknowledgments

This book represents the synthesis of twenty-five years of research, work experience and consulting for each of the primary authors. It integrates best practices from consulting firms, colleagues, non-profits, and clients. We would first like to acknowledge our former employers for providing practical opportunities to learn and build strong skills in global leadership, marketing, consulting, organizational change, large-scale systems change, and strategic thinking, among many others. It was this solid foundation that allowed us to create this methodology.

As a theoretical foundation, we worked with or studied the work of many thought leaders in the fields of leadership development, developmental psychology, integral theory, and others. The theoretical giants on whose hard work we built the Innovative Leadership and Organizational Transformation models include Terri O'Fallon, Ph.D., Susanne Cook-Greuter, Ph.D., Hilke Richmer, Ph.D., Roxanne Howe-Murphy, Ed.D., Ken Wilber, David Kolb, Morgan McCall, Michael Lombardo, Mark Mendenhall, and Allan Bird. These leaders shared not only their theories, but ongoing guidance and encouragement helping to create a solid framework that is comprehensive and theoretically grounded.

Contributing authors who helped to make this book a reality:
Belinda Gore, Ph.D., Mark Palmer, and Melissa Stone, Ph.D.

Friends and colleagues who served as constant cheerleaders and editors, listened to stories and dreams about the book, and helped make it come to fruition. The teachers, trainers, and mentors who taught how to lead—and when to follow.

The Ohio State University Office of International Affairs who inspired the writing of this book and provided ongoing insight.

Clients who participated as case studies, as well as Capital University MBA students who gave feedback on the book by virtue of doing graduate work using the Fieldbook and writing articles that are incorporated into the foundation for this book.

Family who provided continual support and encouragement as well as inspiring us to be thoughtful, dedicated to work, and to contribute to the world in a meaningful way.

Publisher and friend, Russ Volckmann, Ph.D.

Graphic design and layout firm Creative Spot, Copy/Content Editor Sara Phelps, as well as editors, reviewers, endorsers, thought partners, and countless others who spent untold hours making this possible.

Table of Contents

FOREWORD

The *Innovative Leadership Workbook for Global Leaders* is a gift to leaders who are serious about leading effectively in a global context, improving their leadership skills, and running highly effective organizations. As with earlier books in the Innovative Leadership series, this workbook is replete with tools, models, questions, processes, work plans, and reflections about the inner and outer work that's necessary to make personal and systemic change that lasts.

Confronted with a world that is strikingly different from what it was just a decade ago, we face rapidly shifting economic, political, and national security realities and challenges. To respond to these changes, it is essential that our universities and companies build globally competent leaders—that is, leaders possessing a combination of critical thinking skills, technical expertise, and global awareness allowing them to comprehend, analyze, and perform efficiently and effectively in the context of an increasingly globalized world.

For our leaders, global competence and citizenship is an indispensable qualification to work cooperatively in seeking and implementing solutions to significant economic, technological, political, and environmental global challenges. Moreover, global competence is essential to our leaders as they work in an increasingly competitive global marketplace, and to our nation as it addresses its global security needs. The skills that form the foundation of global competence include the ability to work effectively in international settings; awareness of and adaptability to diverse cultures, perceptions and approaches; familiarity with the major currents of global change and the issues they raise; and the capacity for effective communication across cultural and linguistic boundaries.

This workbook is designed to help leaders build those global competencies. It organizes the chaos that accompanies personal transformation and systemic change. It delineates the process into six categories that are straightforward and easy to follow. This workbook gives templates to group the work and offers examples of how this method has worked for a highly successful global leader. And, more importantly, it illustrates and integrates the personal "inside" work of the leader with the "outside" work of the organization. We're introduced to David, a global executive who navigates the Innovative Leadership development process when he is promoted to a higher level role within a global corporation. We are privy to the conversation David has with himself as he applies what he has learned about himself and what he learns about his organization: *What do I do? What do I believe? How do we do this?*

As the vice provost for Global Strategies and International Affairs at The Ohio State University, I can attest to the truth and efficacy of the *Innovative Leadership Workbook for Global Leaders*. Whether you are a university student or a senior executive looking to improve your effectiveness, this workbook provides you with a map that will sometimes take you off the beaten path to places you never imagined or may never have found on your own. The journey is just beginning—embrace it!

—*William Brustein*
Vice Provost for Global Strategies and International Affairs
at The Ohio State University
Winner of the Senator Paul Simon Award for Comprehensive Campus Internationalization

INTRODUCTION
INNOVATIVE LEADERSHIP FOR GLOBAL LEADERS

The national economies of the world have grown to be so integrated and interdependent over the past twenty-five years that a significant number of companies operate today as if the entire world were a single market or entity, comprising many different, interconnected sub-markets, and crossing borders, cultures, time zones, and languages. This high degree of interconnectedness or globalization, brought about through the impact and use of technology, melds with the chaos and continuous change of today's business environment to create a highly dynamic, complex, borderless, multicultural context within which businesses must learn to operate, or suffer the undesirable consequences of being left behind. Organizations must find constructive ways to adapt in order to survive, and the most adaptable organizations will be best positioned to explore all possibilities and to respond with innovative solutions to the complex challenges they face.

Organizations are discovering that globalization demands that leaders master different skills than were required in the past. The world is increasingly characterized by volatility, uncertainty, complexity, and ambiguity (VUCA), and global leaders need new competencies that enable them to respond accordingly. Global leaders deal with intricacies that differ significantly from non-global contexts and must demonstrate cultural adaptability and sensitivity. Yet, many organizations are finding that their supply of global leaders, or even individuals with the potential to become global leaders, does not match the demand. In today's world, the race is not won by the swift, strong, or smart—*the race goes to the most adaptable, those who learn from experience and co-evolve with the complex adaptive systems within which they work and live.*

Leadership plays a critical role in an organization's long-term success, and innovation has become a strategic necessity in today's business environment. In short, global leadership and innovation have a greater impact today than ever before. Despite the volume of resources exploring both leadership and innovation, most approaches provide directional solutions that are merely anecdotal and lack sufficient information to actually allow leaders to make measureable change. Add to this equation the importance of developing global skills, and leaders face an even greater challenge. Technology and increased access to information continue to accelerate the pace of business and of change and organizations are often too overrun with change to handle the torrent of emerging demands.

Questions on how to lead and where to innovate remain puzzlingly philosophically: What is the role of global leadership in a time of looming uncertainty? How will organizations innovate to overcome challenges that are largely unprecedented? In a new climate of business, is there a formula for creating success in both areas?

Designed to help answer those questions for global leaders and help you to perform the critical self-evaluation needed to refine and innovate your own leadership skills, this workbook is fundamentally about global leadership, yet equally an account of applying innovation.

This workbook explores a number of approaches to elaborate on both areas, not just conceptually, but tangibly, by providing exercises designed to enhance your leadership skills. Becoming a better global leader and optimizing innovation jointly hinge on your ability, as a leader, to authentically examine your own inner makeup and diligently address some challenging limitations. Leadership innovation happens naturally and can be accelerated through the use of a structured processes involving your own self-exploration, allowing you to authentically enhance your leadership beyond tactical execution.

Despite their collective value, many conventional applications of leadership and innovation have often proven elusive and even problematic in real-world scenarios. For example, if the leadership team of a struggling organization drives initiatives that focus solely on making innovative changes to incentives, products, and services, without also advancing strategic purpose, culture, and team cohesiveness, they will ultimately miss the greater potential to create a comprehensive turn-around in the organization. Productivity and system improvements are undoubtedly critical, but how employees make sense of their work experience is equally vital to team engagement and commitment. Innovating products and improving functionality—without also creating a better and more meaningful team environment, or a more supportive organizational culture—often appears to pay off in the short term, yet produces lopsided decision-making and shortsighted leadership that create lasting adverse consequences.

Knowing that the future of organizations is irrevocably tied to a world of erratic change, we can no longer afford to improve our systems and offerings without equally advancing our leadership capacity. Leadership empathy and the ability to inspire cultural alignment, along with other important leadership activities, will make a significant impact on your organization and must be implemented as shrewdly as is strategic planning.

Combining global leadership with innovation, then, requires you to transform the way you perceive yourself, others, and your business. By earnestly looking at your own experience—including motivations, inclinations, interpersonal skills, and proficiencies—you can optimize your effectiveness in the current dynamic environment. Through reflection, you learn to balance the hard skills you have acquired through experience with the meaningful introspection attained through deep examination—all the while setting the stage for further growth. In essence, you discover how to strategically and tactically innovate leadership the same way you innovate in other aspects of your business.

Marrying Global Innovation and Leadership

Leadership needs innovation the way innovation demands leadership, and by marrying the two, you can improve your capacity for growth and improved effectiveness. Let's explore innovating leadership in a more tangible way by defining it in practical terms: ***What does innovating leadership really mean?***

It is important first to understand each topic beyond its more conventional meaning. For example, most definitions of leadership alone are almost exclusively fashioned around emulating certain kinds of behaviors: leader X did "this" to achieve success, and leader Y did "that" to enhance organizational performance. Yet behaviors that appear to work in one context may not work so well in another. Even if initially useful, such approaches are still, essentially, formulas for *imitating leadership*, and are likely ineffectual over the long term.

Innovating leadership cannot be applied as a monolithic theory, or as a simple prescriptive measure. It occurs through your own intellect and stems from your own unique sensibilities.

In order to enhance this unique awareness process, you will need a greater foundational basis from which to explore both topics of intellect and sensibilities, which means talking about them in an entirely different context.

Let's start with a straightforward definition of global leadership:

> **Global leadership is a process of influencing people strategically and tactically, affecting change in intentions, actions, culture, and systems within a global context.**

Leadership influences individual intentions and organizational cultural norms by inspiring purpose and creating alignment. It equally influences an individual's actions and an organization's efficiencies through tactical decisions.

Innovation, as an extension of leadership, refers to the novel ways in which we advance that influence personally, behaviorally, culturally, and systematically throughout the organization.

> **Innovation is a novel advancement that shapes organizations: personally, behaviorally, culturally, and systematically.**

In addition to linking the relationship of leadership to innovation, notice that we're also revealing them as an essential part of our individual experience. Just as with leadership and innovation, the way you uniquely experience and influence the world is defined through a mutual interplay of personal, behavioral, cultural, and systematic events. These same core dimensions that ground leadership and innovation also provide a context and mirror for your total experience in any given moment or on any given occasion.

Optimally, then, leadership is influencing through an explicit balancing of those core dimensions. Innovation naturally follows as a creative advancement of this basic alignment. In our experience, leadership and innovation are innately connected and share a deep commonality. Therefore, marrying leadership with innovation allows you to ground and articulate both in a way that creates a context for dynamic personal development—and dynamic personal development is required to lead innovative transformative change.

> Innovating global leadership means global leaders influence by equally engaging their personal intention and action with the organization's culture and systems.

Though we are defining innovative global leadership very broadly, we are also making a distinct point: *The core aspects that comprise your experience—whether they be intention, action, cultural, or systematic—are inextricably interconnected. If you affect one, you affect them all.*

Innovative global leadership is based on the recognition that those four dimensions exist simultaneously in all experiences, and already influence every interactive experience we have. So if, for example, you implement a strategy to realign an organization's value system over the next five years, you will also affect personal motivations (intentions), behavioral outcomes, and organizational culture. Influencing one aspect—in this case, functional systems—affects the other aspects, since all four dimensions mutually shape each other. To deny the mutual interplay of any one of the four dimensions misses the full picture. You can only innovate leadership by comprehensively addressing all aspects.

To summarize, leadership innovation is the process of improving leadership that allows already successful leaders to raise the bar on their performance and the performance of their organizations.

An innovative leader is defined as someone who consistently delivers results using:

- **Strategic leadership** that inspires individual *intentions* and *goals* and organizational *vision* and *culture*;

- **Tactical leadership** that influences an individual's *actions* and the organization's *systems and processes*; and,

- **Holistic leadership** that aligns all core dimensions: *individual intention and action, along with organizational culture and systems.*

The Opportunity of Innovative Leadership

Although the overwhelming focus of today's organizational changes is on system functionality, it is only part of the total picture. Being guided by more strategically inclusive decisions may be the difference between managing failure and creating tangible success. Your leadership must consider a more balanced definition of innovation that comprehensively aligns vision, teams, and systems, and integrates enhanced leadership perspective with system efficiency.

This balanced approach to leadership and innovation is transformative for both you and your organization and can help you to respond more effectively to challenges within and outside the enterprise. Innovating your leadership gives you the means to successfully adapt in ways that allow optimal performance, even within the continual change and complexity of an organization. Conceptually, it synthesizes models from developmental, communications, and systems theory, delivering better insight than singular approaches. Innovative global leadership gives you the capacity to openly recognize and critically examine aspects of yourself, as well as your organization's culture and systems, in the midst of any circumstance.

Defining What an Innovative Global Leader Does

What are specific behaviors that differentiate an innovative leader from a traditional leader? Successful innovative global leaders are ones who can continually:

- clarify and effectively articulate vision, and link that vision to attainable strategic initiatives

- develop himself and influence the development of other leaders

- build effective teams by helping colleagues engage their own leadership strengths

- cultivate alliances and partnerships

- anticipate and aggressively respond to both challenges and opportunities

- develop robust and resilient solutions

- develop and test hypotheses like a scientist

- measure, learn, and refine on an ongoing basis

To further illustrate some of the qualities of Innovative Leadership, we offer this comparison between traditional leadership and Innovative Leadership:

TRADITIONAL LEADERSHIP	INNOVATIVE LEADERSHIP
Leader is guided primarily by desire for personal success and peripherally by organizational success	Leader is humbly guided by a more integrated vision of success based on both personal and organizational performance and the value of the organization's positive impact on both
Leadership decision style is "command and control"—leader has all the answers	Leader leverages team for answers as part of the decision-making process
Leader picks a direction in "black/white" manner—tends to dogmatically stay the course	Leader perceives and behaves like a scientist: continually experimenting, measuring, and testing for improvement and exploring new models and approaches
Leader focuses on being technically correct and in charge	Leader is continually learning and developing self and others
Leader manages people to perform by being autocratic and controlling	Leader motivates people to perform through strategic focus, mentoring and coaching, and interpersonal intelligence
Leader tends to the numbers and primarily utilizes quantitative measures that drive those numbers	Leader tends to financial performance, customer satisfaction, employee engagement, community impact, and cultural cohesion using both quantitative and qualitative measures

What are Learning Practices?

Now that you have this workbook, you may be wondering, "What can I actually do to get better as a leader?" It's one thing to know that you need to "think more strategically," or improve at "giving performance feedback and coaching" to your direct reports. It's something completely different to translate that into practical actions that bring about lasting change, growth, and development.

Since most of us spend over ninety percent of our work time working, rather than in training programs or workshops, time on the job and our day-to-day experience is our best and most accessible opportunity to learn. We just need to know how to use our experience to grow and develop.

Learning practices are actions you can take to accelerate and enhance experiential learning and determine whether you proactively pursue learning in your day-to-day work life, or focus only on getting the job done. Leaders who consistently and rigorously use Learning Practices learn significantly more and faster while achieving better results. The following key Learning Practices have significant potential for growing and accelerating your ability to learn from experience:

LEARNING PRACTICES	RELATED ACTION OR BEHAVIOR
Take responsibility for your own learning and development	Be 100% responsible for the outcome of your engagement with this material
Approach new assignments/ opportunities with openness to experience and positive intention to learn	Each assignment will provide you with opportunities to learn things you did not know about yourself or others; take advantage of these opportunities even if you think you might already know the answers
Seek and use feedback	Identify who will provide you with feedback and use what you discover about yourself to learn and grow (see chapter on Build Your Team)
Develop a clear understanding of your strengths and areas of development	Determine which assessments will give you the most valuable set of feedback (see chapter on Analyze Your Strengths and Situation)
Ask great questions and demonstrate curiosity	Remain openly curious through the process, ongoing learning is an important key to success in leadership development
Listen in a manner that leaves you open to personal transformation	Listen intently, deeply, and empathically identifying ways to not only change your behavior, but also how you see the world
Respond to experience with adaptability and flexibility	Your ability to respond to unexpected situations with finesse will position you well during your development process (see resilience element in Innovative Leadership)
Actively reflect and practice mindfulness	Take the time to answer the reflection questions and be fully present while you are doing the exercises
Actively experiment with new approaches to learning	Find opportunities where you can safely apply new ways of learning skills or behaviors, such as with special projects or in volunteer roles
Closely observe and learn from others	Find a mentor or person you believe has mastered the skills you are trying to develop and closely observe what this person does and how they do it. Try to "steal" or adopt the techniques they use to succeed
Participate as fully as possible	Complete all the exercises to the best of your abilities. Apply the concepts and skills that work best for you, and modify those that do not
Practice good life management	Invest time at scheduled intervals to work on the materials when you are mentally and emotionally at your best
Lean into optimal discomfort; take risks without overwhelming yourself	Be candid, open, and direct. Allow yourself to be curious and vulnerable
Take the process seriously, and more importantly take yourself lightly. Make this a positive and rewarding experience	Allow yourself balance. Find the lesson and humor in both your successes and mistakes. Most importantly, have fun!

To develop the Learning Mindset, use these guidelines:

1. Turn the switch to "on." Decide that you want to develop the Learning Mindset and commit to making it an area of your ongoing growth and development.

2. Be intentional about learning. Use "preflection," orienting yourself toward learning every day by thinking about and envisioning in advance what you want to learn. Use reflection by replaying the day's events in your mind and thinking about what you learned.

3. Use mantras to reprogram your autopilot. All of us operate on autopilot most of the time. This is both a good thing and a bad thing. While it helps to automate repetitive tasks and actions so we don't have to think about them, it also leads us to stop paying attention to important information in the world around us. On autopilot, we work on the basis of old assumptions, beliefs, and data. If you want to start learning more from experience, find your own personal mantra to orient your mind toward learning. Here are a few examples:

    a. "Development is about getting better and better, not being perfect."

    b. "Never give up."

    c. "It's not whether I win or lose. I win if I learn, grow, and develop."

    d. "Observe. Learn. Improve. Getter better."

4. Fake It 'til You Make It. If it doesn't seem natural to you to go through your day with an eye toward learning, one way to counter is to repeatedly and consciously do things that someone with a strong Learning Mindset would do. For example, purposely seek out new experiences that take you out of your comfort zone, and when engaging in those experiences, make it your goal to learn as much as you can through the experience. Over time, you will begin to develop new neural pathways that contribute to new habits of mind and behavior: The Learning Mindset.

To begin using Learning Practices as tools to accelerate and enhance your experiential learning, start with taking responsibility for your own growth and development. Until you actually **own** your development—***taking, not just accepting, responsibility*** for your own learning and growth—you are a passive bystander who is waiting or sleep-walking through life. Unless you take responsibility for your own growth and development, learning may or may not happen, and, if it does, it will be only accidental, incidental, serendipitous, and tacit. And you will be missing out on the biggest developmental arena available to leaders: day-to-day work experience.

As you face the challenges of global leaders, remember that the most effective leaders have the ability to transform their experiences into growth and development. And the greater the challenge, the more significant is the opportunity to develop as a leader. If you have a Learning Mindset and consistently and rigorously put the Learning Practices into action, you will learn significantly more, faster and, as a result, you'll perform at a higher level and create greater value for your company and for yourself.

Adopting the Learning Mindset and using Learning Practices is not as simple as it may seem. As Benjamin Franklin put it in his *New Farmer's Almanac,* "There are three things extremely hard: steel, a diamond, and to know one's self." On the surface, the logic is clear: attitudes lead to behaviors. And, you may already be thinking, "Of course, I have a Learning Mindset! I do some of those Learning Practices all the time!" Unfortunately, most of us do a pretty poor job of assessing our own competencies and capabilities. We tend to exaggerate our strengths and downplay our weaknesses. We all need to use a heightened level of self-examination and conduct an honest appraisal of ourselves as we work on developing ourselves as leaders.

How to Use the Workbook

Each chapter of the workbook builds on a series of exercises and reflection questions designed to guide you through the process of developing your own abilities as an innovative leader. We recommend that you use the following sequence to efficiently process the material:

1. Read Intently

Read through the chapter completely, as we introduce and illustrate an integrated set of concepts for each element in building Innovative Leadership.

2. Contemplate

Using a set of carefully chosen applications and specifically designed exercises will help to bring the concepts to life. Through a process of dynamic examination and reflection, you will be encouraged to contemplate some significant, real-life implications of change. Many of the exercises can be done on your own; others are designed to be conducted with input from your colleagues.

3. Link Together Your Experience

As you sequentially build your understanding, you will begin noticing habits and conditioned patterns that present you with clear opportunities for growth. Though you may encounter personal resistance along the way, you will also discover new and exciting strengths. As you become more adept at using these ideas, you will find yourself increasingly capable of proactive engagement with the concepts, along with an ability to respond to situations requiring Innovative Leadership with greater capacity.

Once you have completed the process, you will have created a plan to grow as an innovative global leader.

Getting the Most from the Workbook

Before you get started, take a moment to think about why you purchased this workbook. Setting goals and understanding your intentions and expectations about the exercises will help you identify and drive your desired results.

In order to help clarify, consider writing your answers to the following questions:

- What are the five to seven events and choices that brought you to where you are professionally and personally?

- What stands out in the list you have made? Are there any surprises or patterns?

- How did these events and choices contribute to choosing to buy and use this workbook?

- What do you hope to gain from your investment in leadership development?

- What meaningful impact will it have professionally and personally?

In addition to reflecting on the questions, we recommend you use the Learning Practices to help you get the most out of this investment in your development. It is our experience that people who adhere to the following practices tend to have a deeper and more enriching overall experience, and more effectively take advantage of what this workbook has to offer.

ASSESSMENT

Innovative Leadership for Global Leaders

Leadership Behaviors

Situational Analysis

Resilience

Developmental Perspective

Leader Type

The following is a short self-assessment to help you identify your own scores relating to Innovative Leadership for global leaders. It is organized by the five domains of Innovative Leadership. This will give you a general sense of where you want to focus your efforts. We encourage you to take this survey as a way to get a snapshot of where you excel and where you may want to focus your energies. Think about the past year when determining your answer. If you are not sure, select "Sometimes," as the survey will not score properly unless you answer each question. The survey should take about 10 minutes to complete.

Assessment Instructions:

- Complete all questions per page. Each of the five sections will appear on separate pages.

- Complete each page and calculate your score on each of the five elements of Innovative Leadership.

Score Yourself on Awareness of Leader Type and Self-Management

Think about how you responded to work situations over the past year and answer the following questions using this scale:

Never (1)   Rarely (2)   Sometimes (3)   Often (4)   Almost always (5)

1. I have taken a leadership type assessment such as the Enneagram, Myers-Briggs Type Indicator, or DiSC, and used this information about myself to increase my effectiveness.   1 2 3 4 5

2. I use the insight from this assessment to understand my type. Specifically, I understand my gifts and limitations, and try to leverage my strengths and manage my limitations.   1 2 3 4 5

3. I have a reflection practice where I understand, actively monitor, and work with my "fixations" (negative thought patterns).   1 2 3 4 5

4. I have a clear sense of who I am and what I contribute to the world.   1 2 3 4 5

5. I manage my emotional reactions to allow me to respond with socially appropriate behavior.   1 2 3 4 5

6. I am aware of what causes me stress and actively manage it.   1 2 3 4 5

7. I have positive coping strategies.   1 2 3 4 5

8. I actively seek ways to feel empowered even when the organization may not empower me.   1 2 3 4 5

Total Score

- If your overall score in this category is 24 or less, it's time to pay attention to your leadership type and self-management.

- If your overall score in this category is 25 to 31, you are in the healthy range, but could still benefit from some focus on your leadership type and self-management.

- If your overall score is 32 or above, congratulations! You are self-aware and using your leadership type to increase your effectiveness.

Score Yourself on Developmental Perspective Aligned with Innovation

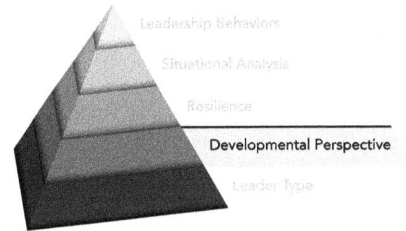

Think about how you responded to work situations over the past year and answer the following questions using this scale:

Never (1)   Rarely (2)   Sometimes (3)   Often (4)   Almost always (5)

1. I have a sense of life purpose and do work that is generally aligned with that purpose.   **1 2 3 4 5**

2. I am motivated by the impact I make on the world more than on personal notoriety.   **1 2 3 4 5**

   1 2 3 4 5

3. I try to live my life according to my personal values.

   1 2 3 4 5

4. I believe that collaboration across groups, organizations, and cultures is important to accomplish our goals.

   1 2 3 4 5

5. I believe that getting business results must be balanced with treating people fairly and kindly.

   1 2 3 4 5

6. I consistently seek input from others to test my thinking and expand my perspective.

   1 2 3 4 5

7. I think about the impact of my work on my community and the world.

8. I am open and curious, always trying new things and learning from all of them.   **1 2 3 4 5**

9. I appreciate the value of rules and am willing to question them in a professional manner.   **1 2 3 4 5**

Total Score

- ◢ If your overall score in this category is 27 or less, it's time to pay attention to your developmental level, including testing your current level and focusing on developing in the area of developmental perspectives.

- ◢ If your overall score in this category is 28 to 35, you are in the healthy range, but could still benefit from some focus on developing in the area of developmental perspectives.

- ◢ If your score is 36 or above, congratulations! Your developmental level appears to be aligned with innovate leadership, yet this assessment is only a subset of a full assessment.

Score Yourself on Resilience

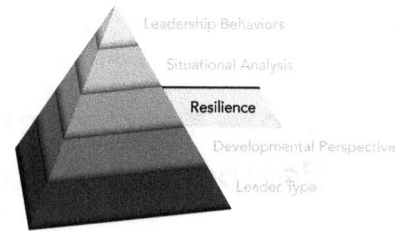

With regard to work situations, think about your level of response over the past year and answer the following questions using this scale:

Never (1)   Rarely (2)   Sometimes (3)   Often (4)   Almost always (5)

1. I consistently take care of my physical needs such as getting enough sleep and exercise.   **1 2 3 4 5**

2. I have a sense of purpose and get to do activities that contribute to that purpose daily.   **1 2 3 4 5**

3. I have a high degree of self-awareness and actively manage my thoughts.   **1 2 3 4 5**

4. I have a strong support system consisting of a healthy mix of friends, colleagues, and family.   **1 2 3 4 5**

5. I can reframe challenges to find something of value in most situations.   **1 2 3 4 5**

6. I build strong trusting relationships at work with a broad range of people. **1 2 3 4 5**

7. I am aware of my own "self-talk" and actively manage it.   **1 2 3 4 5**

8. I have a professional development plan that includes gaining skills and additional perspectives from a broad range of people who think and act differently than I do.   **1 2 3 4 5**

Total Score

- If your overall score in this category is 24 or less, it's time to pay attention to your resilience.

- If your overall score in this category is 25 to 31, you are in the healthy range, but could still benefit from some focus on resilience.

- If your score is 32 or above, congratulations! Although this assessment is only a subset of the full resilience assessment, you are likely performing well in the area of resilience.

Score Yourself on Situational Analysis

Think about how you responded to work situations over the past year and answer the following questions using this scale:

Never (1)   Rarely (2)   Sometimes (3)   Often (4)   Almost always (5)

1. I am aware of my own passions and values.   **1 2 3 4 5**

2. My behavior consistently reflects my goals and values.   **1 2 3 4 5**

3. I feel safe pushing back when I am asked to do things that are not aligned with my values.   **1 2 3 4 5**

4. I am aware that my behavior and decisions as a leader have an impact on the people I work with (even if I am not directly managing them/others).   **1 2 3 4 5**

5. I am deliberate about aligning my behaviors with the behaviors the organization values and I pay attention to delivering the desired results (both results and behaviors).   **1 2 3 4 5**

6. I am aware of how my values align with those of the organization and where they are misaligned; if there are misalignments, I try to find constructive ways address these differences. I am also aware that organization values and behaviors may differ across countries.   **1 2 3 4 5**

Total Score

- ▰ If your overall score in this category is 18 or less, it's time to pay attention to my alignment with the organization and also the alignment of culture and systems within the organization that I am able to impact.

- ▰ If your overall score in this category is 19 to 23, you are in the healthy range, but could still benefit from some focus on alignment.

- ▰ If your score is 24 or above, congratulations! You are well aligned with the organization, and the organization's culture and systems are well-aligned.

Score Yourself on Leadership Behaviors

Think about how you responded to work situations over the past year and answer the following questions using this scale:

Never (1)   Rarely (2)   Sometimes (3)   Often (4)   Almost always (5)

1. I tend to be proactive. I anticipate what is coming next and actively manage it.   **1 2 3 4 5**

2. I focus on creating results in a way that helps me grow and develop along with those who work for me while accomplishing our tasks.   **1 2 3 4 5**

3. I think about the impact of my actions on the organization rather than just getting the job done.   **1 2 3 4 5**

4. I see how my work contributes to organizational success.   **1 2 3 4 5**

5. I deliberately try to improve myself and the organization.   **1 2 3 4 5**

6. I take time to mentor others, even when I am busy (this could be formal or informal mentoring).   **1 2 3 4 5**

7. I consider myself to be a personal learner and I invest time reading and trying new ideas and activities. I am curious.   **1 2 3 4 5**

8. I have the courage to speak out in a professional manner when asked to do something with which I disagree.   **1 2 3 4 5**

9. I accomplish results by working with and through others in a positive, constructive, and culturally sensitive manner.   **1 2 3 4 5**

Total Score

-   If your overall score in this category is 27 or less, it's time to pay attention to my alignment with the organization and also the alignment of culture and systems within the organization that I am able to impact.

-   If your overall score in this category is 28 to 35, you are in the healthy range, but could still benefit from some focus on alignment.

-   If your score is 36 or above, congratulations! You are well aligned with the organization, and the organization's culture and systems are well-aligned.

CHAPTER 1
Elements of Innovative Leadership

Innovative leadership comprises five elements—Leader Type, Developmental Perspective, Resilience, Situational Analysis, and Leadership Behaviors—reflected in Figure 1.1. These five elements are discussed and applied throughout the balance of the book. For each of the five elements, we discuss the concept and then various assessment instruments that can be used to assess your leadership regarding each element. In this chapter, we will define and describe each element of Innovative Leadership and how they interact, and then provide a general framework for innovating how you lead. Later chapters focus in greater depth on the process to develop your leadership, leverage each of the elements, and provide opportunities to use the instruments.

Leadership Behaviors

Situational Analysis

Resilience

Developmental Perspective

Leader Type

Figure 1.1 Five Elements of Innovative Leadership

Theorists have looked at each of these elements separately over many years, and have suggested that mastering one or two of them is typically sufficient for effective leaders. We believe that while that may have been true in a less complex world, it is no longer the case. What is truly unique in this approach to leadership is the overall comprehensiveness of the model. As the twenty-first century unfolds, the most effective leaders will need a much more holistic view than at any other time in history. In short, leadership excellence is a journey and while all five elements in this model may not be mastered, the leader will be working toward mastery of all of them.

Leader Personality Type (or Leader Type)

Part of the challenge in innovating leadership is learning to become more self-reflective and to put that self-reflective knowledge into practice. Looking inside yourself and examining the make-up of your inner being enables you to function in a highly grounded way, rather than operating only from the innate biases that lead to uninformed, reflexive, or unconscious decision-making.

The Leader Personality Type (referred to going forward as Leader Type) reflects your core predispositions and attitudes as a person. Not surprisingly, these attributes critically influence who you are as a leader and how people will experience your leadership. Knowing this is important because it will provide insight into your "default" presence and will also offer you the opportunity to deploy other leadership traits in situationally appropriate ways. One way to observe this is by examining aspects of your inner being that reflect your personality. The Leader Type is an essential foundation of your personal make-up and greatly shapes your leadership effectiveness. There are several useful tools for helping to describe leadership and personality types. Some of these tools are used by a wide range of organizations, e.g., the Myers Briggs Type Indicator (MBTI), DISC, Big Five Personality Test, and the Enneagram. Each of these tools (or models) has particular strengths in their presentations, as well as certain weaknesses. Their overall purpose is to help you make objective sense of your thought and behavior patterns—i.e., your Leader Type—and those of other people.

Self-awareness, the practice of engaging in self-reflection and achieving clarity of insight, being conscious of one's own identity, and the extent to which perceptions about one's self are accurate and compatible with others' observations, play a pivotal role in leadership. Self-aware leaders self-regulate cognitions, emotions, and behavior more effectively depending on the situation, evaluate their impact on others, and possess higher levels of emotional intelligence.

Thus, they become more versatile in their leadership and may perform better. Consequently, successful leader development is foremost personal development. The Enneagram, one of the most comprehensive systems for understanding personality [leader type] and human development, offers considerable merit to support leaders to become more aware of themselves and others.

—Hilke Richmer, *Doctoral Dissertation*

As observed through Hilke Richmer's research project, the Enneagram is one such typing model. We find the Enneagram especially powerful and we discuss it further below and in greater detail in Chapter Three of this book, when we review Leader Type assessments.

Your ability to use deep self-reflection relies on your development of a capacity for self-understanding and self-awareness, both features of emotional intelligence (as we will discuss further in Chapter Two). Both self-understanding and self-awareness allow you to expand your perspective as well as to develop a greater understanding of others. These traits associated with Leader Type support a leader's abilities to manage self, to communicate effectively with others, and to encourage personal learning. It is important to keep in mind that these personality and leadership types are generally traits that are native to your being and generally do not change significantly over the course of your life. This is an essential point: by understanding your type, as well as those of others around you, you can begin to see situations without the bias of your own perceptions. You can develop a clearer understanding, and can thus make more informed decisions with less reflexive behavior. You can learn to deeply understand the inner movements of your strengths, weaknesses, and core patterns. Leadership typing tools like the Enneagram are helpful in promoting this kind of self-knowledge and pattern recognition.

Given that we all have "blind spots" (namely, things about ourselves that we do not see but that others recognize about us); another important way to gain insight about yourself is to seek feedback from trusted colleagues, family members, and/or friends. Getting feedback in a safe way can help you understand your "real self." This is especially true because the way you appear to others can be difficult to appreciate without such feedback or the use of leadership type assessment instruments.

By learning about these patterns, you can gain perspective on your life and start connecting the dots among your different experiences. Most of us have a concept about how we behave, but that idea is likely clouded and not entirely true. One of the hardest things for most people is to see themselves accurately. How astonishing it is to see through the clouds and recognize yourself clearly.

—Roxanne Howe Murphy, *Deep Living*

Learning at this deeper level from your own inner dynamics can offer remarkable insight about areas of life that, in your own personal experience, you may either exaggerate or underemphasize.

Developmental Perspective

In this workbook, we will be talking about **Developmental Levels and Perspective** as the second of the five core elements (Figure 1.1) in developing Innovative Leadership. Developmental Perspective significantly influences how you see your role and function in the workplace, how you interact with other people, and how you solve problems. The term *Developmental Perspective* can be described as how you make meaning or sense of experiences. This is important because the algorithm you use to make sense of the world influences your thoughts and actions. Incorporating these perspectives as part of your inner exploration is critical to developing Innovative Leadership.

We measure Leader Type using the Enneagram and we measure Developmental Perspective using an assessment called the Maturity Assessment Profile [MAP]. It evaluates three primary dimensions: cognitive complexity, emotional competence, and behavior. The MAP is also a sophisticated instrument for identifying and measuring later stage, developmentally advanced leadership. This assessment is referenced in greater detail in Chapter Three when you determine what assessments you would like to take to support your development.

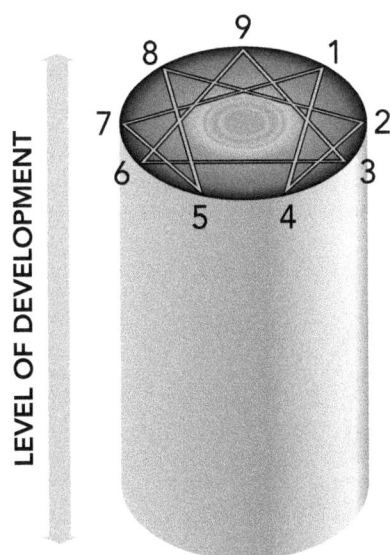

LEVEL OF DEVELOPMENT

Fig. 1.2 Enneagram & Developmental Perspective

In order to connect developmental perspective with Leader Type, let's look at how these two core elements and models come together. While Leader Type is generally constant over your life, you have the capacity to grow and develop your leadership (developmental) perspective. In fact, leadership research strongly suggests that although your inherent Leader Type determines your tendency to lead, good leaders also develop over time. Therefore, it is often the case that leaders are both born *and* made. How leaders are made is best described using an approach that considers their Developmental Perspective. Type remains consistent during your life while Developmental Perspective evolves. This is an important differentiator in leadership effectiveness and allows you to see what can be changed and what should be accepted as an innate personality type.

We can also apply this model at the organizational level to help select and train leaders more effectively. Here are some additional benefits of using a model of Developmental Perspective:

- It guides leaders in determining their personal development goals and action plans using their developmental perspective as an important criterion.

- It is important to consider when determining which individuals and team members best fit specific roles.

- It helps identify high-potential leaders to groom for growth opportunities.

- It helps in the hiring process to determine individual fit for a specific job.

- It helps change agents understand the perspective of others and craft solutions that meet the needs of all stakeholders.

Fig.1.3 Maslow's Hierarchy of Needs

The Developmental Perspective approach is based on research and the observation that, over time, people tend to grow and progress through a number of very distinct stages of awareness and ability. One of the best-known and tested developmental models is Abraham Maslow's hierarchy of needs, a pyramid-shaped visual aid he created to help explain his theory of psychological and physical human needs. As you ascend the steps of the pyramid, you can eventually reach a level of self-actualization.

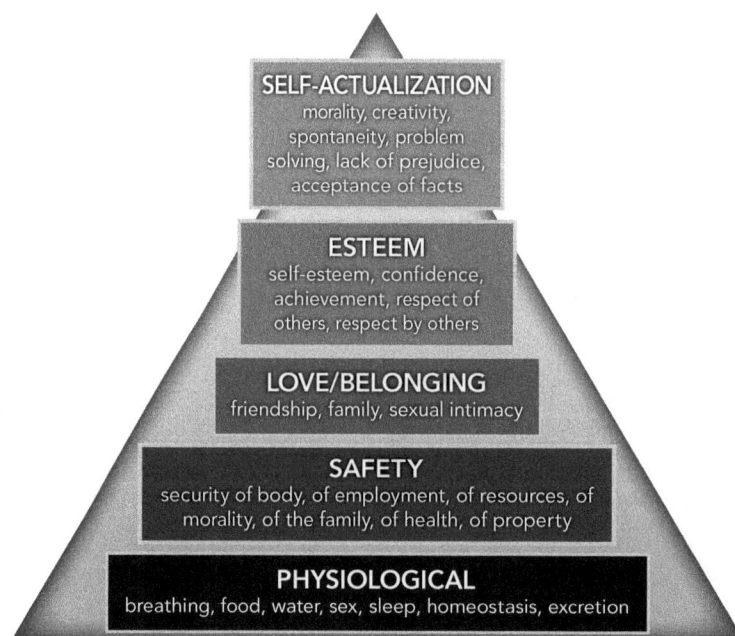

SELF-ACTUALIZATION
morality, creativity, spontaneity, problem solving, lack of prejudice, acceptance of facts

ESTEEM
self-esteem, confidence, achievement, respect of others, respect by others

LOVE/BELONGING
friendship, family, sexual intimacy

SAFETY
security of body, of employment, of resources, of morality, of the family, of health, of property

PHYSIOLOGICAL
breathing, food, water, sex, sleep, homeostasis, excretion

Developmental growth occurs much like other capabilities grow in your life. Building on your Leader Type, you continue to grow, increasing access to or capacity for additional skills. We call this "transcend and include" in that you transcend the prior level/perspective and still maintain the ability to function at that perspective. Using the example of learning how to run to illustrate the process of development, you must first learn to stand and walk before you can run. And yet, as you eventually master running, you still effortlessly retain the earlier, foundational skill that allowed you to stand and walk. In other words, you can develop your capacity to build beyond the basic skills you have now by moving through more progressive stages. It is also important to note that while individuals develop the ability to run, there are many times that walking is a much more appropriate choice of movement. The successful leader has a broad repertoire of behaviors and is able to select the most appropriate one depending on the situation. This concept has been called "situational leadership."

People develop through stages at vastly differing rates, often influenced by significant events or "disorienting dilemmas." Those events or dilemmas provide opportunities to begin experiencing your world from a completely different point-of-view. The nature of those influential events can vary greatly, ranging from positive social milestones like marriage, a new job, or the birth of a child to negative experiences, such as job loss, an accident, or the death of a loved one. These situations often trigger more lasting changes in your way of thinking and feeling altogether. Some new Developmental Perspective can develop very gradually over time or, in some cases, emerge quite abruptly.

Some developmentally advanced people may be relatively young while others may experience very little developmental growth over the course of their life. Adding to the complexity of developmental growth is the fact that the unfolding of Developmental Perspective is not predictably based on age, gender, nationality, or affluence. We can sense indicators that help us identify Developmental Perspective when we listen and exchange ideas with others, engage in self-reflection, and display openness to learning. In fact, most people very naturally intuit and discern what motivates others as well as what causes some of their own greatest challenges.

We believe a solid understanding of Developmental Perspective is critical to innovating leadership and encourage you to delve into this concept in greater detail. The purpose of this workbook is to introduce you to these concepts.

Resilience

Resilience is the third key leadership concept (Figure 1.1) and can be understood in two distinct ways. First, using an engineering analogy, Resilience is viewed as how much disturbance your systems can absorb before they break down. This view highlights the sturdiness of individual systems. Second, from a leadership perspective, Resilience can be viewed as the ability to adapt in the face of erratic change while continuing to be both fluid in approach and driven toward attaining strategic goals. The first definition reflects stability and the second refers to fluidity and endurance. Addressing all aspects of Resilience is critical to optimizing it.

Among the elements essential to leadership, Resilience is unique in that it integrates the physical and psychological aspects of Leader Type and Developmental Perspective to create the foundation of a leader's inner stability. This foundation enables you to demonstrate fluidity and endurance as you adapt to ongoing change.

Fig.1.4 Elements of Resilience

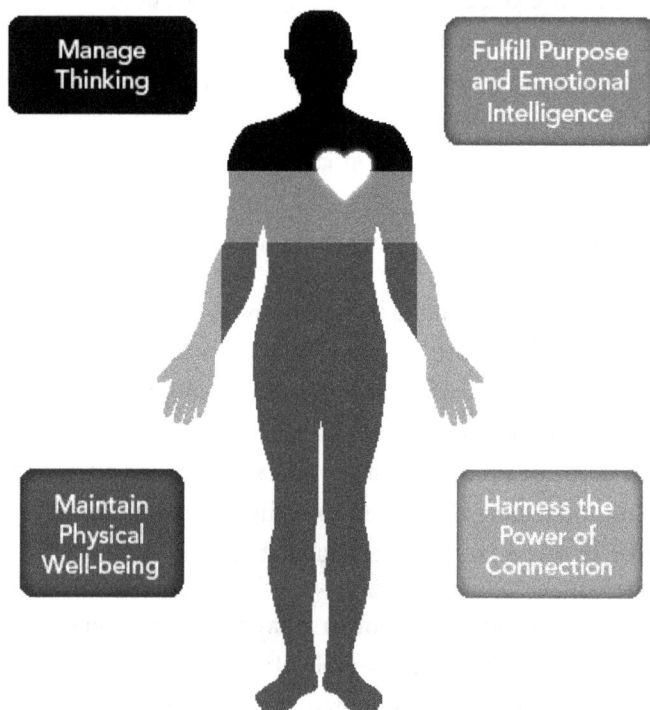

The underlying premise of Resilience is that as a leader, you need to be physically and emotionally healthy to do a good job. In addition to physical and emotional health, the resilient leader also has a clear sense of life purpose, strong emotional intelligence, and strong supportive relationships. For most people, enhancing Resilience requires a personal change.

Our model of Resilience has four categories. They are: maintaining physical well-being, managing thinking, fulfilling purpose using emotional intelligence, and harnessing the power of connection. These categories are interlinked, and all of them must be in balance to create long-term Resilience.

Leaders we work with often initially say they are too busy to take care of themselves. Finding the balance between self-care and meeting all of our daily commitments is tough. Yet, leaders are their own most important instruments of leadership, so caring for oneself is crucial. Most people fall short of their goals and over the longer term make choices *for* Resilience and personal health or *against* it. Our message here is that creating and maintaining Resilience is essential to your success. As you improve your Resilience, you will think more clearly and have a greater positive impact in your interactions with others. Investing in your Resilience supports the entire organization's effectiveness.

The following table provides questions for each of the four Resilience categories to identify opportunities for improvement.

TABLE 1.1 KEYS TO BUILDING & RETAINING PERSONAL RESILIENCE

Maintain Physical Well-being	**Fulfill Purpose and Emotional Intelligence**
Are you getting enough... • Sleep • Exercise • Healthy food • Time in nature • Time to meditate and relax Are you limiting or eliminating: • Caffeine • Nicotine	Understand what you stand for. Maintain focus. Ask: • What is my purpose? • Why is it important to me? • What values do I hold that will enable me to accomplish my purpose? • What opportunities in my professional life do I have that help me achieve my life purpose? • If I were successful beyond my wildest dreams, what would happen?
Manage Thinking	**Harness the Power of Connection**
Practice telling yourself: • Challenges are normal and healthy for any individual or organization • My current problem is a doorway to an innovative solution • I feel inspired about the opportunity to create new possibilities that did not exist before	Practice effective communication: • Say things simply and clearly • Make communication safe by being responsive • Encourage people to ask questions and clarify if they do not understand your message • Balance advocacy for your point with inquiring about the other persons' points • When you have a different point of view, seek to understand how and why the other person believes what they do in a non-threatening way • When in doubt, share information and emotions • Build trust by acting for the greater good

Situational Analysis

Situational Analysis is the fourth core element of our leadership model. Though much of the work of building Innovative Leadership is based on an in-depth examination of your personal and professional experience, understanding the background or context of that experience is equally important. Consider that your experience isn't merely a collection of personal expressions, events, and random happenstance; rather, it is fundamentally shaped by the interplay of your individual attributes, shared relationships, and involved organizations.

Every moment of experience is influenced by a mutual interaction of self, culture, action, and systems. All four of these basic dimensions are fundamental to every experience we have. Situational Analysis involves evaluating the four-dimensional view of reality that is shown in Figure 1.5. This comprehensive approach ensures that all dimensions are aligned, ideally resulting in balanced and efficient action. This balancing without favoring elements is an important skill for innovative leaders.

At their peril, leaders can take a partial or narrow-minded approach to changing organizations. They over-emphasize systems change with little or no consideration to the culture or how their personal views and actions shape the content and success of the change. Situational Analysis enables you to create alignment across the four dimensions on an ongoing basis. This multi-dimensional approach provides you with a more complete and accurate view of events and situations.

Fig. 1.5 Integral Model

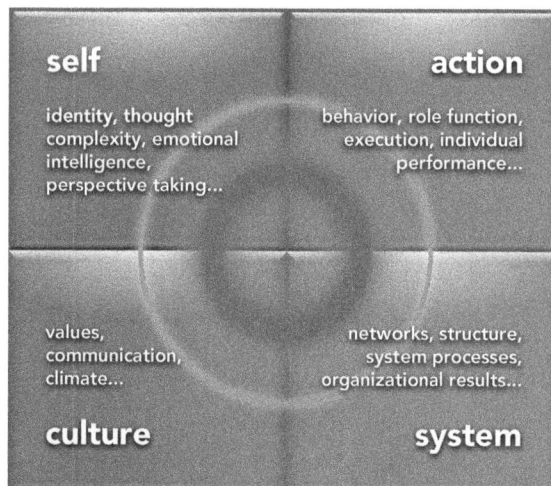

American-born philosopher, Ken Wilber, developed a conceptual scheme to illustrate the four basic dimensions of being that form the backbone of experience. His Integral Model provides a map that shows the mutual relationship and interconnection among four dimensions, where each represents basic elements of human experience.

When you use Situational Analysis, you are cultivating simultaneous awareness of all four dimensions. Let's look at an example. This is a sample narrative taken from *Integral Life Practice* (Wilber et al.) that will give you a more experiential description of how these dimensions shape every situation in your life.

Example: *"Visualize yourself walking into a hospital in the morning…"*

Self *(Upper-Left Quadrant, "I")*: You feel excited and a little nervous about the big meeting today. Thoughts race through your head about how best to prepare.

Culture *(Lower-Left Quadrant, "We")*: You enter a familiar culture of shared meaning, values, and expectations that are communicated, explicitly and implicitly, every day. You understand how things work.

Action *(Upper-Right, "It")*: Your physical behaviors are obvious: walking, waving good morning, opening a door, sitting down at your desk, turning on the computer, and so on. Brain activity, heart rate, and perspiration all increase as the important meeting draws nearer.

System *(Lower-Right, "Its")*: Elevators, powered by electricity generated miles away, lift you to your floor. You easily navigate the familiar environment, arrive at your desk, and log on to the organization's intranet to check the latest global updates on the enterprise software system.

By applying Situational Analysis to organizational leadership as well as organizational change, you would be aware of the four dimensions as referenced above and when leading or changing one, you would consider the impact on the others. If you get promoted and want to be perceived differently, how will you behave in the situation above? What will be different in all four dimensions as you walk into the hospital?

A crucial part of innovating leadership is developing your capacity to be aware of all dimensions of reality in any given moment and to identify misalignments or oversights. Even though you cannot physically see the values, beliefs, and emotions that strongly influence the way an individual colleague perceives himself/herself and the world, nor a group's culture, emotional climate, or collective perception, they still profoundly shape the vision and potential of leaders to innovate.

Situational Analysis is a tool of Innovative Leadership that allows you not only to make more informed decisions, but also helps you optimize performance within yourself, your teams, and the broader organization. The alignment of all dimensions is the key to optimizing performance.

Leadership Behaviors

Let's now shift our focus to the actionable craft of leadership as observable skills and behaviors, and hard skills and their associated behaviors. This involves the fifth core element in our model (Figure 1.1), Leadership Behaviors. Leadership skills and hard skills are critical to success, and serve as objective performance measures of Innovative Leadership.

Hard skills fall into two primary categories: industry-related knowledge, skills, and aptitudes; and functional knowledge, skills, and aptitudes. Leadership skills can be evaluated by observable behaviors and result from knowledge, skills, and aptitudes specifically related to the craft of leadership.

We use the term *Leadership Behaviors* in this workbook when referring to leadership knowledge, skills, and aptitudes and the resulting behaviors. Both hard skills and Leadership Behaviors are critical to building Innovative Leadership; however, the balance between the importance of hard skills and Leadership Behaviors will shift as the leader progresses in the organization, with leadership skills and behaviors becoming increasingly important with career advancement.

Leadership Behaviors are important because they are the objective actions that leaders take to impact organizational success. We have all seen brilliant leaders behave in a manner that damages their organization, and we have seen other leaders continually behave in ways that promote ongoing organizational success. Effective Leadership Behaviors drive organizational success. Conversely ineffective Leadership Behaviors can drive organizational dysfunction or failure. Even the most functionally brilliant leader must demonstrate effective Leadership Behaviors to be successful when leading an organization.

An example of the need for both hard skills and Leadership Behaviors is a client of ours who is a global CIO. To be successful, this CIO must possess the hard skills in technology and administration to understand how the organization operates, and the Leadership Behaviors to be able to effectively lead the people and the organization through difficult change. If either of these sets of skills is missing, the leader and the organization are at risk of failure. Early in his career, a mastery of technology and administration set him apart from his peers. As he progressed into the senior leadership ranks and ultimately to the role of CIO, his use of Leadership Behaviors became his primary focus. While he never lost the need for hard skills, now he relies on his functional and leadership skills to guide his direction and action.

There are different ways to discuss leadership from a skills perspective as demonstrated by Peter Northouse in his book on leadership.

> *There are several strengths in conceptualizing leadership from a skills [actions] perspective. First, it is a leader-centered model that stresses the importance of the leader's abilities, and it places learning skills at the center of effective leadership performance. Second, the skills approach describes leadership in such a way that it makes it available to everyone. Skills are behaviors that we all can learn to develop and improve. Third, the skills approach provides a sophisticated map that explains how effective leadership performance can be achieved.*
>
> --Peter G. Northouse, *Leadership Theory and Practice*

As a leader, it is important to understand the key Leadership Behaviors important to you and your organization. With this understanding, you can determine where you excel and where you may want to refine your skills.

The Leadership Circle Profile (LCP) Behaviors

Fig. 1.6 Leadership Circle Profile

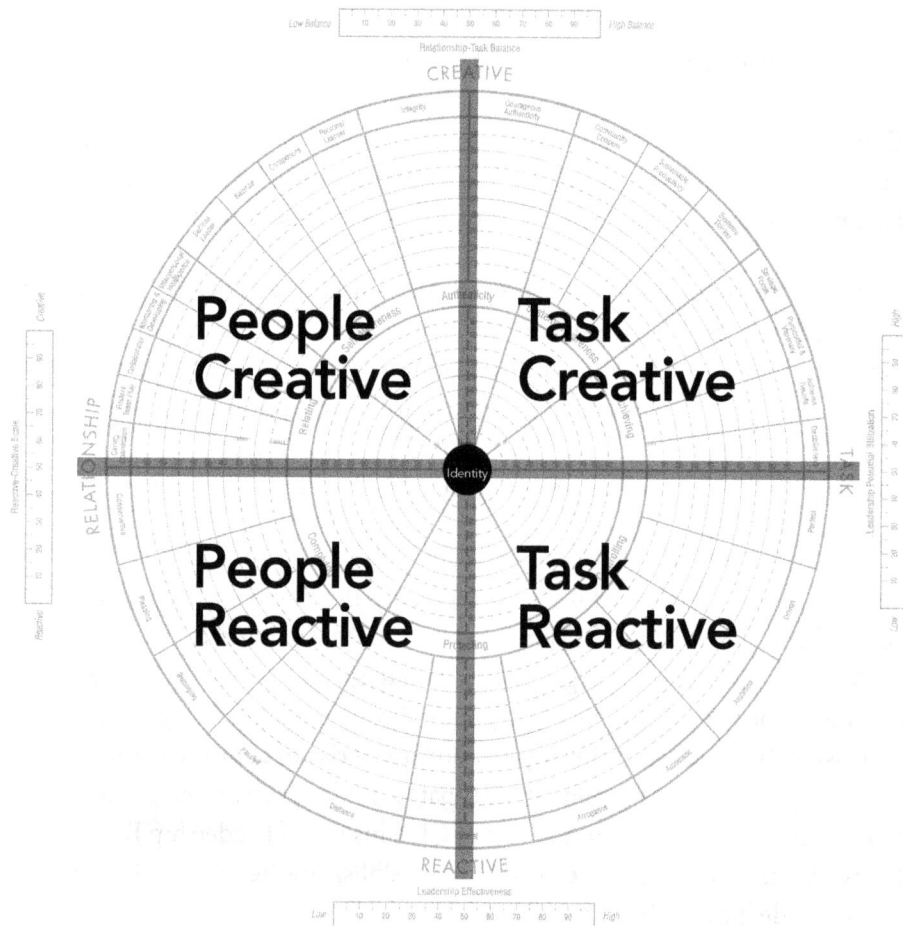

This section discusses overall Leadership Behaviors required for all leaders, and in Chapter Two, we will explore specific Leadership Behaviors that are most important for global leaders.

The Leadership Circle measures key dimensions of leadership shown in the inner circle in Figure 1.6. This model helps assess Leadership Behaviors and helps you determine if your behaviors are creative (proactive) or reactive. We believe that creative behaviors are more effective in most environments and also acknowledge that the specific behavioral requirements are a function of the organization (refer back to Situational Analysis). Reactive behaviors are generally associated with earlier Developmental Perspectives and can be substituted for their more effective "cousins" in the creative categories. The sub-categories in Figure 1.6 are then shown in the outer circle. These are broken into four key dimensions or quadrants: *people creative, task creative, people reactive,* and *task reactive.* These four categories—two creative and two reactive—are created by drawing a line through the circle horizontally to separate the creative (on the top) and reactive (on the bottom) dimensions. The second line is drawn vertically to separate the people dimensions (on the left) from the task dimensions (on the right). The creative behaviors (on the top) consist of various dimensions, such as:

- Relating
- Self-awareness
- Authenticity
- Systems Awareness
- Achieving

These behaviors reflect proactive action and reflect behaviors associated with proactive action that includes setting vision and strategic goals, and coaching and mentoring others to accomplish those goals.

The behaviors in the bottom half of the circle are reactive behaviors. They reflect inner beliefs that limit the leader's ability to be an effective, authentic, and empowering leader. These dimensions reflect behaviors associated with following direction or reacting to circumstances as they arise rather than setting direction and creating the conditions for success.

In this model (Figure 1.6), the creative and reactive dimensions are then split on the vertical axis between people (left) and task behaviors (right). People behaviors are associated with the actions that leaders take to build themselves and their people, such as relating and self-awareness. The task behaviors are actions that leaders take that are associated with the work of running a business, such as systems awareness and achieving. The amount of emphasis on task versus relating will vary depending on your level within the organization, the overall organizational structure, and the organizational type. What is important to note is that leadership requires a balance of task-related behaviors along with relationship-related behaviors and that this balance changes depending on the situation. In this regard, the Leadership Behaviors component of your leadership interacts with the Situational Analysis that we discussed earlier.

It is important to understand the behaviors associated with Innovative Leadership and to have the ability to flex your own Leadership Behaviors to match what is required by the organization. The most effective leaders and organizations demonstrate behaviors that are heavily weighted on the creative end of the scale. The balance between task and relationship will depend, in part, on the role of the leader within the organization. Strong leaders have the capacity to perform both people and task-related roles well.

According to *The Leadership Circle Participant Profile Manual*, "These competencies [behaviors] have been well researched and shown to be the most critical behaviors and skill sets for leaders." Table 1.2 was adapted from *The Leadership Circle Participant Profile Manual*, 2009 Edition, published by The Leadership Circle.

TABLE 1.2 LCP DIMENSION DEFINITIONS

Creative Leadership Behaviors listed below reflect key behaviors and internal assumptions that lead to *high fulfillment, high achievement leadership*.

The **Relating** Dimension measures leader capability to relate to others in a way that brings out the best in people, groups, and organizations. It comprises:

- Caring Connection
- Fostering Team Play
- Collaboration
- Mentoring and Developing
- Interpersonal Intelligence

The **Self-Awareness** Dimension measures the leader's orientation to ongoing professional and personal development, as well as the degree to which inner self-awareness is expressed through high integrity leadership. It comprises:

- Selfless Leader
- Balance
- Composure
- Personal Learner

The **Authenticity** Dimension measures the leader's capability to relate to others in an authentic, courageous, and high integrity manner. It comprises:

- Integrity
- Authenticity

The **Systems Awareness** Dimension measures the degree to which the leader's awareness is focused on whole system improvement and on community welfare (the symbiotic relationship between the long-term welfare of the community and the interests of the organization). It comprises:

- Community Concern
- Sustainable Productivity
- Systems Thinker

The **Achieving** Dimension measures the extent to which the leader offers visionary, authentic, and high accomplishment leadership. It comprises:

- Strategic Focus
- Purposeful and Visionary
- Achieves Results
- Decisiveness

We will use these creative behaviors throughout the book as we refer to Leadership Behavior.

Developing Innovative Leadership

Chapter Two focuses specifically on Leadership Behaviors for global leaders. Chapters 3 through 8 walk you through the process of developing Innovative Leadership, specifically for global arenas. Each chapter reflects one step in the development process and includes tools, templates, questions for reflection, and an example of a person who has completed the process. It is the comprehensiveness of this reflection, coupled with the exercises that will allow you to gain insight into yourself and your organization. This insight is required to change yourself and your organization concurrently or to manage your internal change in the context of an organization that you cannot or do not want to change. It is important to reiterate that leadership development is an ongoing process, a journey. Upon completion of this process, you will be more effective; depending on your goals you may still want to continue developing. Figure 1.7 below shows the six steps.

Figure 1.7 Leadership Development Process

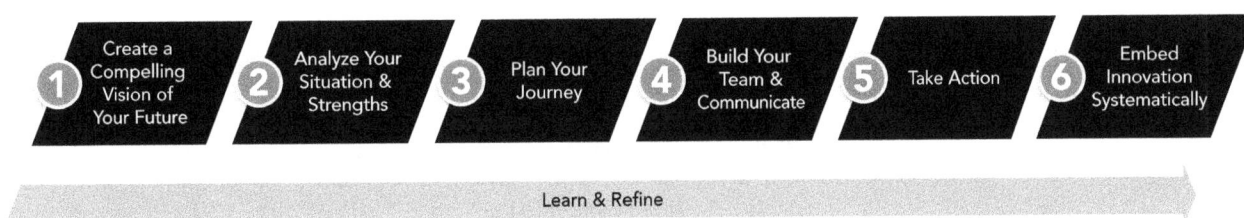

1. Create a Compelling Vision of Your Future
2. Analyze Your Situation & Strengths
3. Plan Your Journey
4. Build Your Team & Communicate
5. Take Action
6. Embed Innovation Systematically

Learn & Refine

While this process appears linear, we have found that when leaders work through these steps, they often return to earlier parts of the process to clarify and sometimes change details they had originally thought were correct. The structure of our process will continue to challenge you to refine the work you have accomplished in prior tasks. Initial ideas are often good ones, but when you work with this tool over time, you will find new insight every step of the way. We encourage you to continue to test your ideas and to feel comfortable going back in the process for further refinement.

The time you spend working on the workbook is an investment in your development. If you are engaging deeply in the process, it will likely take you three to six months or longer to complete. Through this time and thereafter, you will be refining and developing your leadership style, hopefully informed by a strong commitment to improve and a passion for self-awareness and development. Remember that leadership is a journey. Whether managing either personal and organizational change, or internal change alone in the context of an organization that you cannot or do not want to change, reflection and thorough evaluation are required. This reflection will take time and is critical to your growth. We strongly encourage you to engage in the process with as much time and attention as possible. The value you ultimately take from this process is closely linked to the time you invest.

REFLECTION QUESTIONS

What innovative challenges does your organization face?

■■■■■■

How does your organization support effective
leadership for innovation and change?

■■■■■■

In which ways would you consider yourself
an innovative leader?

■■■■■■

How do you personally connect with
leadership and innovation?

■■■■■■

Where are the opportunities for you
to be an innovative leader?

■■■■■■

What would make you and your organization
more effective in leading innovation during a
time of significant change?

■■■■■■

If you were successful beyond your wildest dreams in becoming an
effective leader, what would happen? Write the story as though
it is a newspaper article with your name in the title of the article,
"(Your Name) Has Been Celebrated as a Highly Effective Leader."

CHAPTER 2
Developing an Innovative Global Leader

Because global leadership is often much more complex than domestic leadership, we have dedicated a chapter to discussing the specific leader requirements in a global organization. This chapter calls out some key Leadership Behaviors that are required to focus your attention on the highest impact ones. Some of these behaviors are in addition to those required of an innovative leader in a domestic organization, and they build on what many domestic leaders already do well. We will explore the key competencies associated with working in a global context in either a role in your country of origin with a company that does business globally, or working abroad. Our intent is to provide you with additional information about how to thrive and help you develop global leadership and, by extension, improve the effectiveness of the organization you lead. One of the foundational beliefs of innovating leadership is that the leader is already effectively leading an organization. We will help you build on your already strong foundation.

Global Leadership Competencies

Global leaders require a unique set of leadership competencies to effectively fulfill their roles. These competencies can be categorized by:

(a) cultural awareness and sensitivity

(b) global mindset or perspective

(c) experiential learning

(d) developing and maintaining relationships

(e) communication

The following paragraphs summarize each of the five leadership competencies and provide an example drawn from 2011 interviews conducted by Steve Terrell. These leaders are collectively referred to as "a global leader" to preserve their identities.

Cultural awareness and sensitivity is reflected in awareness and understanding of sensitivity and adapting to cultural differences. It includes being open to differences in various cultures, and having a commitment to learn about other cultures. One global leader described the importance of cultural awareness and sensitivity in terms of understanding "how people in other cultures make decisions, or how they think in terms of the whole process. I found some cultures not straightforward on the decision process." He used Brazil as an example: "People would move around the bushes, but they don't get to the straightforward, logical thinking to make a decision. As I learned the particularities of each culture, it gave me a much better understanding, I think of how to deal with its people."

Some of the behaviors associated with a high degree of cultural awareness and sensitivity include:

- ability to see different perspectives
- capacity for introspection and self-awareness
- interest and excitement for working across multiple cultures and locations
- desire to explore

Having a *global mindset or perspective* goes hand-in-hand with cultural awareness and sensitivity in that it concerns the ability to deal with different perspectives. Each of these different human perspectives is an important reflection of its own cultural context. A global mindset gives one the ability to align and integrate multiple perspectives, and deal with ambiguity and the complexity endemic in global business. One global leader described a global mindset as:

> …having an appreciation for all differences and the value of diversity… recognizing those that you're impacting around the globe…thinking about the value that you can bring when you take in different ideas, instead of focusing on what may be traditionally viewed within one venue. This doesn't only apply to a country or region; it might be within a function because you could have a shallow mindset based on a functional view as well. And I think for me, it's just being very open to others and being able to connect with their ideas—not set aside or dismiss them— you know, giving their ideas value and hearing them out.

Some of the behaviors and characteristics associated with global mindset or perspective include:

- ability to see different perspectives
- ability to align multiple perspectives
- dealing with ambiguity
- dealing with complexity
- being flexible and adaptable
- learning about different ways of doing business
- living outside a comfort zone
- managing multiple priorities
- thinking beyond the borders of one's home country
- understanding the impact of one's decisions on the rest of the world

The need to be good at *learning from experience* is almost a given, as the fast pace, constant change, and inevitable turbulence inherent in the global environment demands that global leaders be agile learners who quickly learn from everything at their disposal and turn every experience into a learning opportunity. These leaders' perspectives are effectively captured in the words of one global leader:

> I think you have to be somebody who is energized by different experiences—and maybe that ties to being a lifelong learner. I'm someone who, despite the fact I don't

have a lot of formal learning, is very curious, intellectually curious, and like to learn. And I think that has been something that has helped me work successfully across multiple cultures and multiple locations, because I see differences as opportunity. I don't see them as something to work, to manage.

The skills of learning from experience involve:

- asking questions
- having an attitude of discovery
- growing through execution against challenge
- learning agility
- learning from mistakes
- listening
- being highly observant, paying close attention
- perceiving and being aware of interpersonal dynamics
- quickly integrating information
- reflection
- willingness to learn

Global leaders also need to be good at ***developing and maintaining relationships***, as they encounter different cultures with different values and find themselves dealing with more complex organizational challenges. This skill involves engaging with people authentically and humbly, with compassion and understanding to facilitate goal achievement through positive cross-cultural relationships. Developing relationships is a necessary and significant investment of time and energy for any leader, but is essential in building relationships in a global environment. Many people from other cultures often value the personal relationships and associated loyalty and commitment that you build with them more than they value efficiency or other Western business values that may be seen as impersonal and less reliable indicators of long-term success.

The specific behaviors and attributes associated with developing and maintaining relationships as a global leader are:

- authenticity
- getting work done through others
- giving people the sense they are valued
- humility
- language skills

Learning another language gives a global leader additional skills for communicating, and so much more. Oftentimes, the structure of language provides an additional view into the intricacies of how the people who speak that language understand the world and make meaning of it in the context of human relationships.

Communication facilitates developing relationships, as well as cultural awareness and sensitivity, and is central to leader effectiveness. The communication behaviors and characteristics associated with global leader effectiveness include:

- building a network
- language skills, including knowledge of nonverbal communication specific to culture
- listening "transformatively/generatively" – deeply, intently, empathically
- asking questions in a non-threatening way with an understanding of how questions may be perceived within a given culture

Innovative Global Leader Development

Although global leader roles require many competencies and capabilities that accrue over time through a wide variety of experiences, including training, education, and other formal development methods, most effective global leaders developed the capabilities they needed to effectively fulfill their role as global leaders through first-hand, personal participation in intensive cross-cultural and global leadership experience that challenged their perspectives and assumptions and stretched their comfort zones. Formal education and training play a role, but are often viewed as secondary in impact and importance to a leader's development compared to hands-on experience in real life situations.

Through their experiences, they gained important new insight, perspectives, and skills in the global leadership competencies discussed earlier. Based on a study (Terrell, 2011), and on an extensive review of other research and global leadership development literature, it is clear that learning from experience is the primary means of developing global leadership competencies.

Early foundational experiences, such as being a sales representative with a multi-cultural clientele, provide important competencies that can be built upon. However, to develop as a global leader, it is important to engage in developmental activities that will challenge, stretch, and transform you both as a leader and as a person. Your best path to develop true global leadership competencies is through:

- intensive, immersive cross-cultural experiences such as work or personal global travel
- hands-on, action-learning-based global leadership development programs
- global or international professional conferences
- overseas site visits
- learning another language
- short-term work and project assignments
- holding global jobs, without relocating to another country or culture
- holding global jobs, after relocating to another country or culture
- relocating to another country to take a new non-global job

It is important to note that you don't have to move or live in a country other than your native country to have significant cross-cultural experiences. Many valuable developmental experiences involve short-term assignments, visits, or projects that involve little travel. Experiences such as global leadership development programs, professional meetings, global travel, and short-term site visits can all have profound and prolonged positive impact on your development as a global leader. The common element among the experiences involved in developing as a global leader is that you develop by gaining first-hand, direct, and personal cross-cultural and global leadership experiences and that these experiences challenge and stretch you both as a leader and as a human being.

How to Learn From Experience

It won't be enough to just participate in these experiences; you also have to engage in them in a certain way. Global leaders who are highly effective actively and intentionally learn from their day-to-day experience. They apply what they are learning to new challenging situations and continue learning as they go forward. Unfortunately, the ability to learn from experience is something that many leaders take for granted or outright ignore. However, if you consistently practice the skills and tactics of experiential learning, you will be significantly better equipped to deal with the complexities and challenges of global leadership.

To get the most out of your day-to-day experiences, keep in mind these two key ideas: The Learning Mindset and Learning Practices. These two elements of learning from experience go hand in hand: The Learning Mindset (attitude) leads to Learning Practices (actions).

What is "The Learning Mindset"?

Think of a mindset as a habitual or characteristic mental attitude that determines how you will interpret and respond to situations. In the context of learning from experience, Learning Mindset is an attitude that predisposes you to be open to new experiences, to believe you can and will learn, and to intentionally grow and develop from your experience. It includes the set of assumptions and beliefs that govern how you think about and approach experience and opportunities, and whether you generally see them as opportunities to learn and develop, as well as your emotional state or feeling about learning, learning situations, and new experiences.

It's helpful to think of Learning Mindset as a set of prescription eyeglasses through which you view the world and your experience. If you operate with a mindset that leads you to view work projects or tasks as things that you need to do in order to fulfill your job responsibilities and to succeed, then you will most likely focus on producing the desired results "on time and under budget," using your current knowledge and skills to accomplish the goal. Now, these are good things to achieve. But if you operate with a Learning Mindset that leads you to view work projects and tasks as opportunities to learn something new, you will focus on expanding your current knowledge and skills as you take creative action to produce the desired results. The conceptual lens of Learning Mindset leads you to see every experience as an opportunity to learn, grow, and develop.

Leaders who have a Learning Mindset see opportunities to learn in all aspects of their work life, and tend to learn more than those who are closed to learning. Leaders whose attitude or stance toward learning embody:

- a belief in their own learning and growth potential
- openness to experience
- motivation, willingness, and desire to learn
- curiosity about others and how they do what they do
- an attitude of discovery and exploration
- an intention and willingness to gain something positive from experience

In summary, an individual in a global role at the "Leader" stage typically will be characterized by the following:

- *Cultural awareness and sensitivity* that allows for understanding and adapting to cultural differences.

- Having a *global mindset or perspective* to deal effectively with different perspectives, and demonstrates the ability to align multiple perspectives, deal with ambiguity and complexity, and become comfortable outside of a comfort zone.

- A strong ability to *learn from experience* and a predisposition to be open to new experiences, to believe in the possibility of learning, intentionally growing and developing from experience, and turning every experience into a learning opportunity.

- *Developing and maintaining relationships* and the ability to engage with people authentically and humbly to facilitate goal achievement through positive cross-cultural relationships.

- *Communication* through which a strong network of relationships is built based on trust, asking questions, and listening "transformatively/generatively," i.e., deeply, intently, and empathically.

Beginning with Chapter Three, we explore how you can use the six-step Innovative Leadership Development Process to improve your effectiveness at this specific stage and also how you might guide others in their development.

REFLECTION QUESTIONS

Do you observe the differences between people of different cultures? If you look around your offices, how many people were born in foreign countries or speak a language of their ethnic origin?

■■■■■■

Do you know and understand the different business customs of your colleagues and clients, and how those may impact your organizational success?

■■■■■■

What specific actions do you employ to learn from your experiences?

■■■■■■

What characteristics of a Learning Mindset do you personally demonstrate?

CHAPTER 3
Step 1: Create a Compelling Vision of Your Future

This workbook for international leaders is designed to provide a step-by-step process to support you in developing your own Innovative Leadership capacity. The fieldbook that serves as the foundation for this workbook has been tested with a broad range of clients as well as hundreds of working adults participating in an MBA program.

The comprehensiveness of these exercises coupled with reflection exercises will give you the insight into yourself and your organization needed to make substantive personal change. While this process appears linear, we have found that when leaders work through these steps, they often return to earlier parts of the process to clarify and sometimes refine their answers. The structure of our process will continue to challenge you to refine the work you have completed in prior exercises. First ideas are often good ones, yet when you work with this tool you will continually find insight. We encourage you to continue to test your ideas and feel comfortable circling back for further refinement.

These tools differ from many others by directing you through an exploration that takes into account your unique, individual experience while simultaneously considering the groups and organizations to which you belong.

The full process is shown below. You are starting on the first step in the process: Create a Compelling Vision of Your Future.

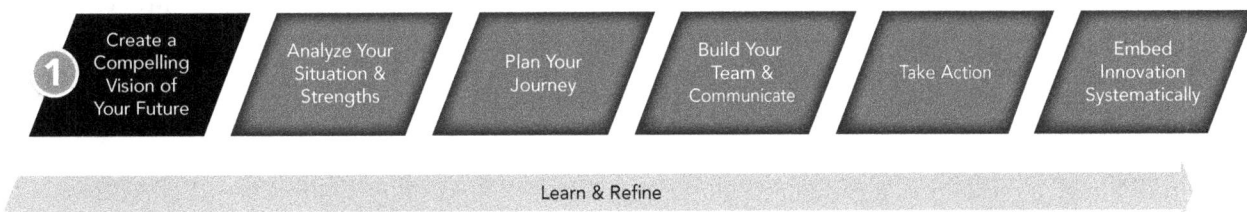

| 1 Create a Compelling Vision of Your Future | Analyze Your Situation & Strengths | Plan Your Journey | Build Your Team & Communicate | Take Action | Embed Innovation Systematically |

Learn & Refine

A starting place for your development process is cultivating a sense of clarity about your overall vision, which can also be summarized as your direction and aspirations. The intention behind your aspirations fuels both personal and professional goals, as well as giving a sense of meaning to your life. When your actions are aligned with your goals, they drive the impact you create in the world at large. As you move forward in the visioning process, we will guide you to begin thinking about individuals or groups who inspire or have a significant influence on you.

Simply put, your vision and aspirations help you decide where best to invest your time and energy. Clarifying vision and values helps you define a manner of contributing to the world that authentically honors who you are. Your vision and aspirations further help you clarify what you want to accomplish over time. You can select the time span that resonates for you, whether short-term—one to five years—or perhaps a longer-term time horizon, such as the span of your lifetime. After clarifying your own unique, personal vision, you will have the foundation for your ensuing change process. Knowing your vision and values creates the basis for your goals and can help you align your behavior with your aspirations.

As part of the visioning process, it is important to consider the context of your leadership role, your organization, or employer. If you are clear about your personal vision, you can evaluate where and how you fit within that organization. On the other hand, if your vision differs significantly from what you do and how you work, the additional knowledge will guide you in finding a role that is a better fit (this transition may not happen in the short term). By knowing your vision and aspirations, you are equipped with information that helps you align the energy you invest with the work you do.

In addition to creating a well-defined vision, it is also important to be clear about your motivation. The combination of vision and desire is what will enable you to maximize your potential. Without sufficient desire, solid vision, and understanding of your current capabilities, you are likely to struggle when progress becomes difficult.

Tools and Exercises

The exercises will guide you in identifying what is most important to you. First, you will define your future, and from that vantage point, clarify your vision and values. You will then consider what you want to do professionally, as well as the type and extent of the impact you want to have on the world.

It is important to note that many people who participate in this exercise will still not have a clearly articulated vision—this is because defining personal vision requires a great deal of introspection for many people. While some people grow up knowing what they want to do for a living, for others identifying a vision is a process of gradual exploration and will take more time and energy than completing a single workbook exercise. You will likely refine your vision as you progress through later chapters in the workbook, based on the information you learn about yourself. Because the visioning process is iterative in nature—a process of self-discovery—the exercises in this book will serve as the foundation for a longer process that may take considerably more time to complete. It will likely change as you gain experience and as your introspective process matures.

Define Personal Vision

Follow the steps defined below:

Step 1: Create a picture of your future. Imagine at the end of your life looking back and imagining what you have done and the results you have created.

- What is the thing you are most proud of?
- Did you have a family? If so, what would they say about you?
- What did you accomplish professionally?
- What would your colleagues say about you?
- What would your friends say about you?
- What relationships were most fulfilling?

For the rest of this exercise, let that future person speak to you and help you set a path that enables you to look back with pride and say things like, "I feel fulfilled and at peace. I lived my life well."

Step 2: Write a story. Now that you have an image of what you will accomplish, write a brief story about your successful life. Include details about the questions above. Make it a story of what you went through to accomplish each of the results for the questions you answered. What you are trying to create is a roadmap for your journey that gives you greater insight into what you would want if you had the option to design your perfect life.

- Who helped you along the way?
- What did you enjoy about your daily life?
- Who was closest to you?
- What feelings did you have as you accomplished each milestone along the way?
- How did you mentor and contribute to the success of others?
- What did you do to maintain your health?
- What role did spirituality or religion play in your journey?
- What job did you have?
- What role did material success play in your life?
- What type of person were you (kind, caring, driven, gracious)?

Step 3: Describe your personal vision. Given the story you have written and the qualities you demonstrated as a person, write a two to five sentence life purpose statement about your highest priorities in life and your inspirations. This statement should capture the essence of how you want to live your life and project yourself.

> ***An example*** *- I develop myself to my greatest capacity and help others develop and thrive in all aspects of their lives. I am wise, conscious, compassionate, and courageous, and contribute to making the world a better place.*

Step 4: Expand and clarify your vision. If you are like most people, what you wrote is a mixture of selfless and self-centered elements. People sometimes ask, "Is it all right to want to be covered in jewels, or to own a luxury car?" Part of the purpose of this exercise is to suspend your judgment about what is "worth" desiring, and to ask instead which aspect of these visions is closest to your deepest desire. To find out, before going on to the next one, ask yourself the following question about each element: If I could have it now, would I take it?

Some elements of your vision don't make it past this question. Others pass the test conditionally: "Yes, I want it, but only if..." Others pass, but are later clarified in the process. As you complete this exercise, refine your vision to reflect any changes you want to make.

After defining and clarifying your vision, it is time to consider your personal values. The combination of these two exercises will help you create the foundation of what you want to accomplish and the core principles that guide your actions as you work toward your vision.

Checklist for Personal Values

Values are deeply held views of what we find worthwhile. They come from many sources: parents, religion, schools, peers, people we admire, and culture. Many go back to childhood; others are taken on as adults. Values help us define how we live our lives and accomplish our purpose.

Step 1: Define what you value most. From the list of values (both work and personal), select the ten that are most important to you—as guides for how to behave, or as components of a valued way of life. Feel free to add any values of your own to this list.

PERSONAL VALUES CHECKLIST

- Achievement
- Advancement and promotion
- Adventure
- Arts
- Autonomy
- Challenge
- Change and variety
- Community
- Compassion
- Competence
- Competition
- Cooperation
- Creativity
- Decisiveness
- Democracy
- Economic security
- Environmental stewardship
- Effectiveness
- Efficiency
- Ethical living
- Excellence
- Expertise
- Fame
- Fast living
- Fast-paced work
- Financial gain
- Freedom

- Intellectual status
- Leadership
- Location
- Love
- Loyalty
- Meaningful work
- Money
- Nature
- Openness and honesty
- Order (tranquility/stability)
- Peace
- Personal development/learning
- Pleasure
- Power and authority
- Privacy
- Public service
- Recognition
- Relationships
- Religion
- Reputation
- Security
- Self-respect
- Serenity
- Sophistication
- Spirituality
- Stability
- Status

PERSONAL VALUES CHECKLIST (CONT.)

- Friendships
- Having a family
- Health
- Helping other people
- Honesty
- Independence
- Influencing others
- Inner harmony
- Integrity

- Time away from work
- Trust
- Truth
- Volunteering
- Wealth
- Wisdom
- Work quality
- Work under pressure
- Other: _____

Step 2: Elimination. Now that you have identified ten values, imagine that you are only permitted to have five. Which five would you give up? Cross them off. Now cross off another two to bring your list down to three.

Step 3: Integration. Take a look at the top three values on your list.

- How would your life be different if those values were prominent and practiced?

- What exactly does each value mean? What do you expect from yourself, even in bad times?

- Does the personal vision you've outlined reflect those values? If not, should your personal vision be expanded? Again, if not, are you prepared and willing to reconsider those values?

- Are you willing to create a life in which these values are paramount, and help an organization put those values into action?

Now, which *one item* on the list do you care most about?

Putting Vision into Action

After defining and clarifying your vision and values, the next step is to reflect on how to put them into action. You will consider the things you care about most as well as your innate talents and skills to determine what about your current life you would like to refine or change. You are probably passionate about specific interests or areas within your life; if you're really fortunate, you will have opportunities to participate in one or more of those areas.

You likely have passions that will always remain in the realm of hobbies. The purpose of this exercise is to consider how best to incorporate your passions into how you make a living, and the goal is to move closer to identifying your passions and expressing them in as many areas of life as possible.

In our experience, part of figuring out what you want to do is paying attention to what you find profoundly interesting. Those interests simply reveal themselves in the course of your daily interaction with peers and colleagues, and quite frequently at business functions. They are reflected in whatever you find yourself reading; they even display themselves in the context of more casual occasions, and are often seen in activities shared among friends.

This type of exercise appears very simple on the surface, but may be something you revisit annually in order to refresh what is genuinely important to you. We find that revisiting allows you to nurture a sense of continual clarity about your direction and iteration provides a mechanism for clarifying your direction as you grow and develop. With everything you try (false starts and all), you will discover a deeper truth about yourself that moves you closer to your most authentic passions. Some of those passions will be incorporated into your career; other passions shape your personal life.

Exercise: Putting Vision into Action

Step 1: Identify your foundation. Answer the three questions below by compiling a list of responses to each.

- What are you passionate about? This will come from the prior exercise and should now be relatively concise.

- What meets your economic needs?

- What can you be great at?

Note: your answers to these questions should reflect your values from the Personal Values Checklist.

Step 2: Review and identify overlap. Review your answers and identify the overlaps.

Step 3: Harvest the ideas. Based on the overlaps, do you see anything that might be incorporated in what you do or how you work? This could mean adding an additional service line to an existing business or allocating a portion of your work time to a project that aligns with your values.

An example of this is a client who, based on significant reflection, learned he valued giving back to the community in a way that he was not doing at the time. He was the CEO of a technology firm and though born and raised in India, his passion was offering computer training for returning U.S. veterans. Even though he maintained the job of CEO, he added a community support function into his business. His passion for service to the community and professional skills afforded him the ability to follow his passion and still run a successful business. In the process of following his passion, he is building the workforce in his community and building his reputation as a civic leader and successful entrepreneur.

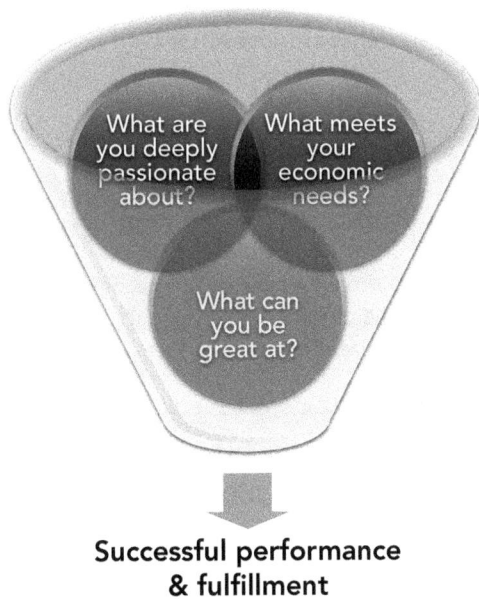

What are you deeply passionate about?

What meets your economic needs?

What can you be great at?

Successful performance & fulfillment

Vision-Based Actions

Innovative Leadership Reflection Questions

To help you develop your action plan, further clarify your direction using the reflection questions below. "What do I think/believe?" reflects your intentions. "What do I do?" reflects your actions. "What do we believe?" reflects the culture of your organization (i.e., work, school, community), and "How do we do this?" reflects systems and processes for your organization. This exercise is an opportunity to practice Innovative Leadership by considering your vision for yourself and how it will play out in the context of your life. You will define your intentions, actions, culture, and systems in a systematic manner.

Table 3.1 contains an exhaustive list of questions to appeal to a broad range of global leaders and you will likely find that a few of these questions best fit your own personal situation. Focus on the questions that seem the most relevant. We recommend you *answer one to three questions* from each category.

TABLE 3.1: QUESTIONS TO GUIDE THE LEADER AND ORGANIZATION

What do I think/believe?

- How do I see myself in the future? What trends do I see around me that impact this view? Have I considered how these trends impact the way I want to contribute?
- How does my view of myself impact me? Am I inspired by my vision? Terrified?
- How do I see myself within the larger environment (this can range from my family, the organization, to the international environment)?
- How do I gather input from key stakeholders to incorporate into my vision (family, business, self)?
- After doing the exercises, what is my vision?
- After doing the exercises, what are my values? What do I stand for? What do I stand against?
- What are the connections between my business vision and my personal mission, passion, and economic goals?

What do I do?

- How do I research trends that will impact my industry so I can understand my future placement and how to navigate potential transitions in my industry?
- How do I synthesize competing goals and commitments to create a vision that works for me in the context of the communities I serve (family, friends, work, and international community)?
- How do I develop my vision taking greater economic conditions into account?
- What do I tell others about my vision? Do I have an "elevator speech"? Is it something I think is inspirational?
- When others observe me living my vision and values, what observable behaviors do they see?

What do we believe?

- How does my personal vision fit within the larger context of my family, my community, my industry, or my job?
- How do I create a shared belief that my vision will help the organization succeed within the larger community and also help the community succeed?
- What do we believe we stand for as an international organization? How should we behave to accomplish what we stand for (guiding principles/values)? Do my values align with the organizational values?
- How do I reconcile differences between my values and those of my organization? How will these differences impact my ability to develop toward my vision and goals?

How do we do this?

- How do I monitor the organization's impact on my vision? How do I honor my vision when helping define/refine the organizational vision?
- What is our process for defining/refining changes to our shared vision for the organization and other systems I function within? What is our process for clarifying and documenting our values? How do I ensure that my values are aligned with our guiding principles?
- Who gives me feedback on their perspective of my progress? How often? What form would I like this feedback to take?
- What measures help me determine progress toward my vision and values? How do I track and report progress toward these goals? Is my behavior supporting the organizational goals? Are the organizational goals supporting my goals?

To support your success in this workbook, we provide an example of a composite of multiple global leaders whom we call David. David tests as a "Level 5 Leader," so his answers reflect that level of thinking and perspective taking. His completion of many of the exercises, work sheets, and reflection questions give you an example of how a successful international leader might use this process.

Introduction to David

This case study is a composite, but draws heavily from the personal and professional experiences of our co-author, Ben Mitchell, and his colleagues.

In his late 50s, David was recently promoted to a global management role as sales manager for a large global corporation. He is doing the workbook to help him identify the leadership changes he needs to make to succeed in his new role.

He first joined his current company in 1990 as a lab technician and was promoted to a senior chemist where he formulated high performance coatings for the fenestration industry before he assumed the position of Global Technical Service Manager, Extrusion Coatings in 1997. From 1999-2002, David was a product manager for a competitor before rejoining his current employer in 2003.

In his current role, he manages the fenestration coatings business for residential and commercial building products including R & D, sales, and marketing for the Americas as well as oversight for international markets.

A member of the American Institute of Architects and the Construction Specification Institute, David served on the technical committee of the National Fenestration Ratings Council. He serves as chair of the Finishing Task Group for Aluminum Materials for the American Architectural Manufacturers Association. In this role, he guides the committee in writing coating specifications for window, curtain wall, and commercial construction industries. He also serves on the technical committee for the Window and Door Manufacturer Association and is a member of the Glass Association of North America. As a delegate for the Council on Tall Buildings and Urban Habitat, he attends their global seminars and meetings.

Vision

My vision is to grow personally and professionally by utilizing scientific education and my business experiences, and to support the success of others. I am a committed husband, father, and grandfather and live my values in all areas of my life.

Values

- achievement
- expertise
- working well under pressure

Now David will answer reflection questions from each category. He shares these answers with you because reflection is one of the more important skills that all leaders must develop. One important element of this workbook is that as a developing leader, you have the opportunity to see inside the thought process of a successful global leader. It is rare that many leaders share their inner thoughts and feelings, and it's valuable for you to see how others approach these questions.

REFLECTION QUESTIONS

What do I think/believe?

- *How do I see myself in the future?*

   I see myself as a person who can significantly contribute to this organization through my extensive technical experience in formulating, as well as in application dynamics. While taking on a global role brings considerable challenges—including working at a level of management that is new to me—it is very exciting and I feel my years of global travel in other roles will serve me well. Few people have had the opportunity to travel the world and experience as many cultures as I have. Although the time away from home can be difficult, the rewards are many. Even difficulties in logistics, language, and simple things like ordering meals become an adventure and learning experience.

   The trend is toward globalization of the business community. We can no longer live as an island in today's business world and I choose to embrace this new paradigm by taking a leadership role. By doing this, I feel I can positively impact my company as well as the industry as a whole.

- *After doing the exercises, what are my values? What do I stand for? What do I stand against?*

   My top personal values are achievement, expertise, and working under pressure, and I remain true to the solid business principles that I exhibit in the U.S. despite different business practices in some other parts of the world. Recognizing that in some parts of the world values and ethics may vary, I consider it a must to keep all interactions legal and ethical according to my standards.

What I stand for remains constant with good business practices by treating all suppliers, customers, employees, and even competitors fairly and as I would like to be treated. While I remain loyal to my personal ethical standards, I must respect the differences in all cultures where I travel and do business.

While I'm unable to control these as I work with international companies and groups, I stand against unethical business practices and, most importantly, human rights violations. My greatest hope is that I can be a positive influence on ethical and moral business practices that could create a positive work environment for all.

What do I do?

■ *How do I gather input from key stakeholders to incorporate into my vision (family, business, self)?*

I have a strong sense of my personal vision and values that have developed over many years and were shaped by my upbringing.

My family could not support me financially going to college, but I had great emotional support from them and for that I am forever grateful. I have never been the smartest person, but what I learned by putting myself through college has motivated me to teach the next generation the importance of work ethic and commitment to excellence. I learned to lead by example, and I never asked anyone do more than I was willing to do. As an example, an MBA program will not likely benefit my career at this stage, but my participation has encouraged others who were hesitant to continue their own education by showing them that if I could do this, so can they.

When I think about how I work with others, I rely very heavily on developing mutual respect between myself and my business associates. Part of the balance is to take into account the background and culture of the people you are dealing with—one of the more difficult skills to learn. For example, in Japan, there is a very rigid and structured hierarchy that dictates who is allowed to speak and even where each person sits during a meeting. In the U.S., with few exceptions, employees at any level are comfortable in giving an opinion of what you or the organization is doing wrong. For each region, I try to study as much as I can to learn what is expected and allowable from managers before dealing with them and certainly do an extensive investigation before traveling to a new country. Within this context I can then best relate these stakeholders to those with whom I have done similar work knowing that this industry, with some regional cultural bias, works the same around the world. Regardless of nationality or culture, all people want to be treated with respect for their beliefs and opinions. This is not difficult, but does take some commitment.

■ *How do I develop my vision taking additional economic conditions into account?*

I have been successful in my career by doing the right thing in all situations. My vision is constant irrespective of economic conditions, but my course of action will vary. I have relocated several times and taken different jobs because economic conditions changed. I am very aware that in our industry, changing conditions have a make or break impact on any given region.

I must always be aware of the fluid and dynamic macroeconomic status of the world and the microeconomics in each region of the world. For example, the Middle East may be building not only to improve the lives of their people now, but with an eye toward an infrastructure and economy for decades in the future in the event the oil industry loses its economic power. Understanding what drives business in a region is important because even though the global economy may be slow spending money for resources that a region has now is critical to prepare for the future. China, on the other hand, may consider an eight percent growth rate a major issue because it is a significant slowdown from what they are used to even though most of the world would be thrilled with that growth rate in today's market. Within this context, even in the United States different region have very different economic conditions. For example, a trigger may cause New York City to slow slightly while the Florida market nearly stops. Staying aware of economic conditions is very important in knowing where to put time and resources to be most effective. This current role will require that I am highly aware of economic variations as my decisions will impact the company's success, and also the careers and lives of the people working for and with me. It is imperative that I am continually monitoring macro and micro trends (overall economy and our industry).

What Do We Believe?

■ *How do I create a shared belief that my vision will help the organization succeed within the larger community and also help the community succeed?*

I think buy-in from all stakeholders, including management, coworkers, direct reports, and labor is critical and must share in understanding that the goal is that we all succeed or fail together. If you cannot clearly communicate the vision as well as the benefits of accomplishing that vision to all parties, you are destined to fail as some will view your plan as a selfish one and not support it, some may even work against it. Creating buy-in can be achieved many ways, but it must start with open communication and with all parties aware that not everyone will agree. What is key, however, is making it clear that everyone's input is important and will be taken into consideration. Once the plan, approach, and the perceived benefit to all is laid out to everyone, you will need to address the concerns of those not in agreement. You then must let them know you understand their concerns and will monitor the program with their concerns in mind and, if needed, will adjust as we must always be flexible with changing markets and time. With this explained, you want to get them to verbally commit to supporting your plan for the good of the team and community.

I also acknowledge that people will disagree on occasion and we may "agree to disagree" and still move forward. While I prefer consensus, I realize that I may need to balance time investment in creating buy-in and speed of action. This is a tough call and is the "art" of leadership.

- *What do we believe we stand for as an organization? How should we behave to accomplish what we stand for (guiding principles/values)? Do my values align with the organizational values?*

This is a critical concern when dealing with organizations and cultures around the world. As a company, we consider safety and environmental stewardship as key business principles. As a company, our business principles are based on our values. Wherever we operate, we aim for the highest standards of performance and behavior in everything we do. We have a clear list of behaviors that are expected, a subset includes: free enterprise, integrity, community involvement, and open and honest communication. These principles and values, and corresponding policies and procedures, provide a solid guide to how we behave and also how we do not behave.

My organization's core values align very well with mine as we always look to be good community members and strive to understand and embrace diversity in all forms. The days of doing business with people that "look like me" and "think like me" are over. To be successful, you don't have to agree with others' beliefs, but you must be tolerant and accepting. What we all agree to as a company are the values and practices we use to accomplish our goals. I am proud to be working for a company that holds such high ethical and business standards.

How do we do this?

- *How do I monitor the organization's impact on my vision? How do I honor my vision when helping define/refine the organizational vision?*

I should have already evaluated and confirmed that my vision is in alignment with the organization, or it would be very difficult for me or the organization to be successful. At times, I have had to reconsider my vision as the company changed management or philosophy, but have always understood the business needs for the change and was able to adapt my attitudes and behaviors still holding true to my vision and values. In addition, my personal vision has helped shape the division's vision. This is important in today's business environment as we become more of a global society with changing markets and economies to which we must adapt. If for some reason the new corporate vision was unacceptable to me, for my personal happiness and success as well as for the good of the company, I should consider making a change to an organization that had a compatible vision with mine. It would be tough to be fully engaged in my work, particularly as a leader, if the organization's vision were incompatible with my personal vision.

I honor my vision by taking what I have learned in many years of international travel and communicating this by honoring others' beliefs and ideas. I have seen colleagues go to different regions of the world and say, "Now that I am here, you need to change to the American way of thinking because it is best." Often, people go on to ridicule the cultural beliefs of locals because they are so foreign and different. Some Americans believe that those who come to the U.S. to work should know our language and adapt to our culture, but when doing business abroad see no reason to adapt to local culture. When looking at a global organization's vision, this is one of the foundations you must understand and incorporate in order to succeed. This philosophy has been a differentiator in my success over the years of working internationally.

■ *Who gives me feedback on their perspective of my progress? How often? What form would I like this feedback to take?*

Feedback takes many forms from staff to management to customer with variations based on their paradigm of experiences and expectations. With regional managers being in other parts of the country and world, communication becomes critical and issues must be addressed in a timely manner. Delaying discussion of issues only makes them more intense so that a relatively minor concern festers into a major issue. With management, again, constant contact on an as needed basis is required, but for me I know what is expected and rarely need feedback as I go about executing a plan. Everyone is different. I have some reports who, although excellent performers, need constant reinforcement and feedback to maintain a greater level of confidence.

Customers fall into many different categories of required information. Some, for example in the Middle East, want feedback and support almost daily, and if not followed through, may be disappointed or even get angry. However, some other cultures as long as the material we are supplying is correct and without delay, would rather not be bothered to get or give feedback. One phrase I tell my group that is very simple and speaks volumes about how a company, organization, or department operates is: "Do we adapt to our customers' needs whether internal or external, or do we make our customers adapt to us?" If we can work to adapt to their needs and be the easiest to work with, our odds of being successful increase greatly.

While the type and volume of feedback varies significantly, I personally value feedback greatly and adjust my behavior based on the feedback when necessary. In some cases, feedback may come in a nonverbal form rather than spoken or written words. I have honed my skills to be perceptive about feedback and ask for it when appropriate. The other thing I believe is important about feedback is that I follow-up and let people know what I am doing/have done with the information they provided.

Creating a Compelling Vision for Yourself

Now that you have read David's personal narratives, it is time to complete the exercises and answer the questions for yourself. We encourage you to complete all of the exercises as they establish a strong foundation for your personal vision, values, and course of action; so, be patient and give yourself time to explore your hopes and dreams as authentically as possible. You will know you've completed this step and are ready to move to the next when you feel you have created a vision and set of values that truly inspire you.

Throughout this chapter, we have discussed exercises that will help you clarify your life direction and create a compelling vision for your own life and work. The next chapter focuses on assessing where you are now in your career and personal development.

Define personal vision and values

What do I think/believe?

What do I do?

What do we believe?

How do we do this?

CHAPTER 4

Step 2: Analyze Your Situation and Strengths

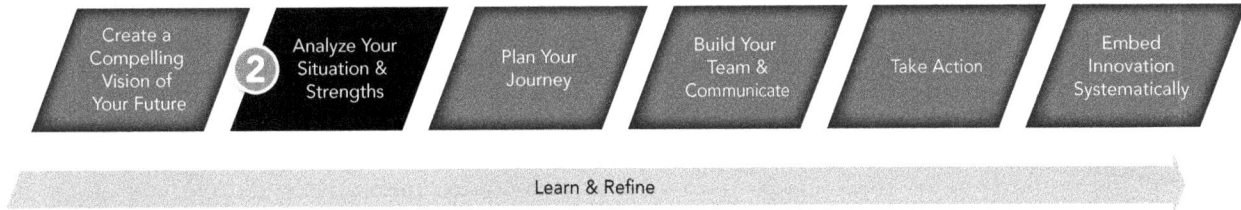

| Create a Compelling Vision of Your Future | ② Analyze Your Situation & Strengths | Plan Your Journey | Build Your Team & Communicate | Take Action | Embed Innovation Systematically |

Learn & Refine

Now that you have developed (or refined) your vision, it is time to examine your strengths and development opportunities. This step will help you refine and clarify those strengths and weaknesses using standard assessment tools. You will then decide which areas you would like to improve by building on what you already do well and addressing weaknesses. We recommend using a general guideline that focuses eighty percent of your effort on building your existing strengths and twenty percent on addressing weaker areas. Though this a general approximation, the 80/20 rule is a directional one stemming from the belief that you are already successful and have simply taken the opportunity to further advance and refine your capabilities. If you find serious deficiencies, those deficiencies can be best addressed by other leadership books and resources.

It is important to combine your vision with a firm understanding of your current performance, abilities, and personality type. The data will help you become more aware of your strengths and weaknesses, and also clarify how others see you. The combination of information will help you determine the gap between your current state (based on assessment data) and your vision.

It is important to note that many people have a higher capacity than they are able to use at work. This could be caused by working in a job that does not use your full abilities. When you begin taking assessments, it will be important to get information from a broad range of sources to ensure you have a clear and accurate picture of your true capacity.

Assessment Tools

One of the primary ways to help you understand your current development and performance is using a combination of assessments to measure your current skills and abilities along with your personality style and developmental perspective. This should allow you to identify the gap between your present state and what you need to fulfill your vision.

Several good assessments are available. The tools we suggest have been used extensively with our clients and are recommended with a high degree of confidence. We find that each provides vital information in helping to convey a comprehensive picture of strengths, weaknesses, and opportunities. These assessments are aligned with the five elements of Innovative Leadership

Leadership Behaviors

Situational Analysis

Resilience

Developmental Perspective

Leader Type

discussed in chapter one. Some are expensive and require a skilled coach to interpret them; however, we know this option is not practical for everyone. Metcalf & Associates has created a free online assessment that does not replace the detailed assessments recommended below, but does offer a high-level view of your Innovative Leadership and can indicate key areas of focus. It can be accessed by going to http://www.metcalf-associates.com/innovative-leadership-assessment.html.

The tools we use to help develop global innovative leaders are:

◼ Leader Type Assessment - Enneagram

We recommend using the Enneagram first and foremost to *discover your own personality type* and, as appropriate, to determine the types of those with whom you interact. The Enneagram is used for personal growth, relationships, therapy, and in the business world as an indicator of an individual's primary personality type. The *Riso-Hudson Enneagram Type Indicator* (version 2.5) provides a reliable, *independently scientifically validated* tool for that purpose. Finding your type is not the final goal, but merely the starting place for working with our system, and embarking on a fascinating and rewarding journey of self-reflection.

The Enneagram helps you to see your *own* personality dynamics more clearly. Once you are aware of the importance of personality types, you see that your own style is not equally effective with everyone. One of the Enneagram's most useful lessons is how to move from a style of interacting in which others are expected to mold themselves to your way of thinking/values to a more flexible style in which you act from an awareness of the strengths and potential contributions of others. By doing so, you help others become more effective themselves—and as a result, harmony, productivity, and satisfaction are likely to increase (source: www.enneagraminstitute.com/practical.asp). The Enneagram is an inexpensive assessment that is available online and does not require a certified coach to interpret.

◼ Developmental Perspecitve - DEV:Q Job Style

We recommend using the DEV:Q™ Job Style Assessment to better understand your fit for role or the unique patterns you use to translate information, manage tasks, and engage in teams. This assessment falls into the category of developmental perspective on the Innovative Leadership pyramid and helps you better understand how your style fits into different job roles. These patterns correlate to capabilities needed at key levels of work common to all organizations. Based on over 50 years of social-behavioral research, the DEV:Q™ algorithm evaluates your performance style along a spectrum (efficiency drives versus innovation drives), and classifies your capability into one of four performance levels and nine prototypes, each with a dominant inclination toward specific types of tasks, roles and outcomes. The DEV:Q™ Job Style Assessment is very cost-effective, with twenty-four questions and only twenty minutes to take online.

- **Developmental Perspective - MAP**

We recommend the Maturity Assessment Profile (MAP) to evaluate developmental perspective. Dr. Susanne Cook-Greuter developed this assessment to describe developmental perspectives as part of her Ph.D. at Harvard University. It is widely considered one of the most rigorously validated, reliable, and advanced assessment tools used to evaluate adult leadership development. Participants taking the assessment complete thirty-six sentence stems about various topics. The freeform response format allows test takers to provide a wide range of information which gives the scorer ample data to evaluate varying developmental features along three main lines: cognitive complexity, emotional affect, and behavioral. The combination of the three allows the scorer to determine the action logic, or how people tend to reason and respond to life. It is critical for you to be completely open and honest when taking this assessment in order for there to be sufficient data to provide an accurate score. The MAP assessment is available through Pacific Integral (www.pacificintegral.com) or Susanne Cook-Greuter (www.cook-greuter.com). This assessment requires a coach to interpret the data and comes with a detailed report explaining the developmental levels and the perspectives each offers.

- **Resilience Assessment**

Metcalf & Associates created a basic tool to help you assess your attitudes and practices that help support resilience, and identify areas where you can further build your capacity. It is based on fundamental stress management research including the characteristics that support "stress hardiness," a concept pioneered by Suzanne Kobasa. This assessment can be found at http://www.metcalf-associates.com/resilience-assessment-tool.html.

- **Leadership Behaviors - The Leadership Circle Profile (LCP) Competency-Based 360° Assessment**

It is important for a leader to have an accurate view of what others see to be able to make appropriate changes and gauge the impact of these changes. This tool looks specifically at a set of well-researched Leadership Behaviors as key levers to drive success, and not only allows you to identify possible behavioral changes, it can also help you improve your self-awareness by specifically understanding how others see you. It is this ability to see what others see that will allow you to target your behavioral changes and fine-tune your effectiveness. The Leadership Circle is available at www.theleadershipcircle.com and requires a certified coach to administer and provide feedback.

It is important to note that how others perceive you is, in part, based on their own values and overall view of the world. Interpreting that data can be just as much an art as scientific inference. Rather than taking such feedback at face value, we suggest trying to understand those evaluations as well as the culture of the organization. For example, if an individual is very results-oriented in a culture that prefers collaboration, that individual may be perceived as having a negative disposition—controlling, driven, and autocratic. Another organization with a culture that is more aligned with a results-driven approach may perceive that very same individual as being extremely positive—achieves results, vision-focused, and system-oriented. Part of understanding development and effectiveness is finding the organization aligned with your leadership style, as well as a culture that can support your potential to grow.

◢ Global Leadership Competency Assessment

There are several assessment instruments that global leaders can use to gain a better understanding of their current level of capability and readiness to fulfill the demanding role of global leader. The Global Competencies Inventory (GCI) (The Kozai Group, Inc., 2008), the Global Mindset Inventory (GMI) (Javidan et al., 2007), and the Global Executive Leadership Inventory (GELI) (Kets de Vries et al., 2004), three well-known assessment instruments utilized in global leadership development, each focus on different, specific sets of global leadership competencies. We recommend you consider using one of these assessments to specifically test your global leader behaviors and competencies.

Future Projections

We find that reading futurist publications for specific industries is very helpful. The role of the futurist is to evaluate current trends and build possible scenarios for how the future might unfold. By building on our capacities for leadership, we can use these scenarios as part of our planning process to provide insight into overall societal trends, ensure we are well prepared for the potential impact of ever-changing business conditions, and suggest imminent scenarios that help you navigate those trends effectively.

Several organizations provide very effective views into the future. One that we regularly reference is The Arlington Institute (TAI), founded in 1989 by futurist John L. Petersen. It is a nonprofit research institute that specializes in thinking about global futures and creating conditions to influence rapid, positive change. They encourage systemic, non-linear approaches to planning and believe that effective thinking about the future is enhanced by applying emerging technology. TAI strives to be an effective agent of advancement by creating intellectual frameworks and toolsets for understanding the transition in which we are living.

By understanding the trends, you can align your development plans with future trends. If your industry is in flux over the next five years, your plan should prepare you to develop at a rate at least as fast as the industry and preferably much faster so you can lead rather than follow your industry change.

Tools and Exercises

Now that you have reviewed the tools and taken some or all of the assessments, it is time to synthesize what you have learned about yourself through a Strengths, Weaknesses, Opportunities, and Threats worksheet (SWOT) and through a series of reflection questions. For the SWOT analysis, please complete the worksheet below.

TABLE 4.1: SWOT ANALYSIS

Strengths	Opportunities
What sets you apart from most other people?	*What opportunities are open to those who have these strengths?*

Weaknesses	Threats
What do you need to improve?	*Do you have weaknesses that need to be addressed before you can move forward? Do any pose an immediate threat such as losing your job?*

David's Development Journey Continued

David will now walk through his worksheets and journal entries for analyzing his situation and strengths. David took the Enneagram assessment and tested primarily as a Type Eight, Challenger. This is a typical type for senior executives, so his innate qualities are likely well aligned with the organization's leadership personality. He also took the developmental perspective assessment, the MAP. He scored at the Strategist level of development, which puts him in the top five percent of all leaders on this scale.

SWOT WORKSHEET ANSWERS

Strengths

What sets you apart from most other people?

- Over 10 years of technical experience in industry
- Advanced chemistry and technical courses
- Traveled internationally for 18 years
- Given many technical and industry presentations to international groups
- Participated in global strategy planning

Opportunities

What opportunities are open to those who have these strengths?

Technically qualified people with good people skills and willing to travel are hard to find and, if committed to top level performance, have many opportunities

Weaknesses

What do you need to improve?

- I need more patience with people not working up to their potential
- Time management is, and has been, a struggle. Being considered a workaholic that travels extensively makes it challenging to balance personal and business lives

Threats

Do you have weaknesses that need to be addressed before you can move forward? Do any pose an immediate threat to you, such as losing your job?

- I do not believe I have weaknesses at this time that would pose significant threats
- A threat might be not delegating enough; I get overwhelmed when I should be pushing regional managers to accept more responsibility that would allow them to grow professionally

---

Innovative Leadership Reflection Questions

To help you develop your action plan, it is time to further clarify your direction using reflection questions. The questions "What do I think/believe?" reflect your intentions. "What do I do?" questions reflect your actions. "What do we believe?" reflects the culture of your organization (i.e., work, school, community), and "How do we do this?" reflects systems and processes for your organization. This exercise is an opportunity to practice Innovative Leadership by considering your vision for yourself and how it will play out in the context of your life. You will define your intentions, actions, culture, and systems in a systematic manner.

Table 4.2 contains an exhaustive list of questions to appeal to a broad range of readers. Find a few that fit your own personal situation, and focus on the questions that seem the most relevant to you. We recommend that you *answer one to three questions* from each category.

TABLE 4.2: REFLECTION QUESTIONS

What do I think/believe?

- Given the direction the world is unfolding, how do you believe you are positioned to be a leader in the future?

- Are you able to balance professional and personal commitments? How does your leadership style impact your ability to meet your overall life goals?

- How has your leadership style contributed to the organization's success? Have you done things that did not produce the results you had hoped? How would you change to produce different results?

- How would you like to impact the people who work for you? Have they grown and met their career goals while working for you? What have they contributed to the organization while working for you?

- If you are leading a change initiative, what will you need to change to lead this effort effectively? Will you lead the same way this time or will you change from what you have done in the past?

What do I do?

- How do you play to your strengths?

- How do you mitigate the threats?

- What opportunities do you want to take advantage of and what do you need to do to position yourself for success?

- How do you compensate for significant weaknesses?

- What assessments are you taking to gather objective data about your performance (this could include performance appraisals, developmental assessments, 360° feedback, or informal feedback from multiple sources)?

- How do you communicate your personal changes and your sense of urgency to those around you who may be impacted by these changes?

What do we believe?

- Notice the various people and groups in your life (family, colleagues, boss, community, friends, etc.) and what they report as "urgent" right now

- Anticipate how they will interpret your development and change. How will they talk about it? Specifically for your organization, how will the changes you aspire to make impact your constituents?

- Determine how your sense of urgency connects with the group's sense of urgency based on its priorities, goals, and pain points

- How does the culture of your support system impact your beliefs about yourself and about leadership? Would these beliefs change if you changed who you spent time with?

- Based on developmental perspectives, where is the cultural center of gravity in your support system? How are people with more open or broader perspectives perceived? How are people with earlier or smaller perspectives perceived? How will this impact your ability to change?

- What are the cultural barriers to you changing? What are the cultural enablers? Will your changes be aligned with the organizational culture? Will they send a message that you do not value the culture?

How do we do this?

- What systems and processes are enablers and barriers that will impact my development?

- What processes and measures alert us to urgency in our system that we need to tend to? What are the early warning signs?

- What processes measure your progress? Are you progressing as measured by criteria that will increase your professional effectiveness? Are you progressing against your personal standards? How will your support system or organization reward or punish your changes based on the measures?

- Do the measures indicate a sense of urgency to you that support focusing on development?

David's Reflection Responses

We will now walk through David's answers from each section of Table 4.2. Simply follow along with David and answer his questions for yourself, or select questions that fit your current situation.

What do I think/believe?

- *Given the direction the world is unfolding, how do you believe you are positioned to be a leader in the future?*

  I believe my years of global travel in a technical role have given me experience that has prepared me for success. This technical background gives me the knowledge base to communicate with all facets of our business, and my experience gives me creditability and respect in meetings with other facilities around the world as well as with customers, and, although not required for my position, has been very important in my success. Having travelled and conducted business in developing nations with different religions and cultures, I am well equipped to keep an open mind and adapt to situations as they arise. You do not need to compromise your beliefs nor ethics to be accepting and tolerant of others; you just need an open mind. As the business world evolves into a more global society, you simply cannot keep your mind closed to others if you are to continue to be successful.

- *How would you like to impact the people who work for you? Have they grown and met their career goals while working for you? What have they contributed to the organization while working for you?*

  I think I have had a very positive impact on people working for me by seeing that hard work and commitment pays off—you just may need to be patient because it doesn't happen overnight. Several of my reports have followed my path of a very strong technical background and applying it to become experts in the field. We are continuing our professional growth by taking advanced business classes together to give us the tools to better apply our technical knowledge and experience. With this path, I think they have or will meet or exceed their career goals. With this personal and professional growth, my team has grown the business significantly both in top line sales, income, and customer satisfaction that has been an integral part of our success.

What do I do?

- *How do you play to your strengths?*

  If you look at my SWOT analysis, you will see that years of global travel and technical expertise are key strengths. From this, I have been able to give technical papers to global leaders in my industry that have opened doors I otherwise could have never opened.

- *How do you take advantage of opportunities?*

  My team and I are not viewed just as sales or business people, but as expert resources in our field whose credibility has been earned and is respected. Being a technical expert is only one part of the equation; you must also have the personal skills to communicate and execute plans. We work hard to refine and deliver plans.

- *How do you appropriately respond to your personal sense of urgency while supporting the organizational objectives?*

  In today's business world, you are only as good as your last P & L or review and I understand this and act accordingly. I strongly feel, I cannot consider myself very successful if I obtain my personal goals but the organization does not meet its goals. My personal sense of urgency to succeed must include making sure the organizational goals are met. For example, if the company decides an emerging market is where we must grow to meet our overall objectives, then I will need to modify my personal focus and urgency to support this. If, for some reason, I find myself not aligned with their goals for personal reasons, I would seriously consider moving to an organization that better aligns with my beliefs.

What do we believe?

- *Anticipate how your change will be interpreted. How will colleagues talk about it? Specifically for your organization, how will the changes you aspire to make impact your constituents?*

  I believe most people in my organization, although resistant, understand that change is part of life and they must embrace it or risk becoming irrelevant and/or unneeded. As long as an explanation is given, why it is needed, and the perceived benefit of the change, nearly all will adapt and support. There will be some water cooler talk about changing something from the way it's been done for decades. This is where cooler heads must prevail and not respond in kind, but stay on message that this change is critical for the future and show each how this long term can benefit them in their position. To help get buy-in from my organization, I listen to their concerns and make sure they understand I am serious about their concerns, and that if they give me full support and it does not work as planned, will include them on revising plan if needed.

How do we do this?

◼ *Which systems and processes are enablers and barriers that will impact my development?*

We use a variety of personnel evaluation tools monitored through supervisory mid-year and annual review processes. Everyone writes the objectives for personal and team growth and development each year along with the business goals. We each then do a self-evaluation with several criteria at mid-year and year-end.that are then commented on by the immediate supervisor. We then go through a peer review process to assure that all evaluations are rated fairly and consistently. Although this peer review process can be difficult, it does give a sense of fairness and uniformity to all participants. This enables all to understand and agree with what is expected of them so they can stay on track with their career. The biggest barrier might be that the peer review only takes place formally once per year, but I have an open dialogue on a regular basis with both my supervisor and reports and would never allow an issue to fester until the next review. I believe the year-end is a time to review and formalize what has taken place, and would rarely be a time to bring up a major new issue that needs attention.

◼ *Which processes and measures alert us to urgency in our system that we need to tend to? What are the early warning signs?*

E-mail or voicemail questions that go unanswered for too long, or answers that are incomplete and not well thought through are signs of a problem. Frequent interaction, whether face-to-face or via electronic media, should allow a manager to get a sense of how people are doing. With the daily challenges we face in a global competitive market where face-to-face meetings are rare, no communication electronic or otherwise is a red flag that something is not going well. It may be that someone is trying to take on too much and feels overwhelmed, doesn't want to bother me, or feels that any issue may be looked down upon. Any of these are issues I need to be made aware of or this person will not be working up to their potential and risk becoming unhappy in their job which will magnify the underlying problem. Waiting on production or sales numbers to evaluate someone's performance can be dangerous as a minor issue might have developed into a crisis by the time it shows in reports. Regardless of your industry, you are in the people business and understanding and managing people, regardless of culture and background, will be your biggest challenge and reward.

Your Process of Evaluating Your Situation and Strengths

Now that you have followed David's responses, it is time to complete the worksheets. Based on your assessment results, if you have not done so already, complete the SWOT analysis in Table 4.1 and *answer one to three questions* from each section for yourself. By internalizing your strengths and opportunities, you can identify the gaps that, when filled, will help you to accomplish your vision. Understanding your weaknesses will also help you know what to avoid, what to improve, and what personal feedback to request from people skilled in those areas.

We encourage you to complete all of the exercises, taking your time and giving proper attention to gathering input from several different sources. When you have a clear picture of your strengths and opportunities, you will be ready to move to the next step. You may now find that you have a different or clearer perception about where you excel and how those areas can complement your vision.

This chapter helped you clarify your strengths and weaknesses as a foundation for your personal transformation journey. Bear in mind that you are creating your own story through this process. The next chapter focuses on the framework for creating a development plan that will allow you to close the gap between your vision and where you are today.

Resources

- **Enneagram:** www.enneagraminstitute.com

- **DEV:Q Assessment Tools:** www.laborgenome.com

- **Mature Adult Profile Assessment (MAP):** www.pacificintegral.com

- **The Leadership Circle 360° Assessment:** www.theleadershipcircle.com

- **Resilience Assessment:** www.metcalf-associates.com

- **Innovative Leadership Assessment:** www.metcalf-associates.com

- **Susanne Cook-Greuter Research:** www.cook-greuter.com

- **Terri O'Fallon Research (StAGES Model):** www.pacificintegral.com

What do I think/believe?

What do I do?

What do we believe?

How do we do this?

CHAPTER 5

Step 3: Plan Your Journey

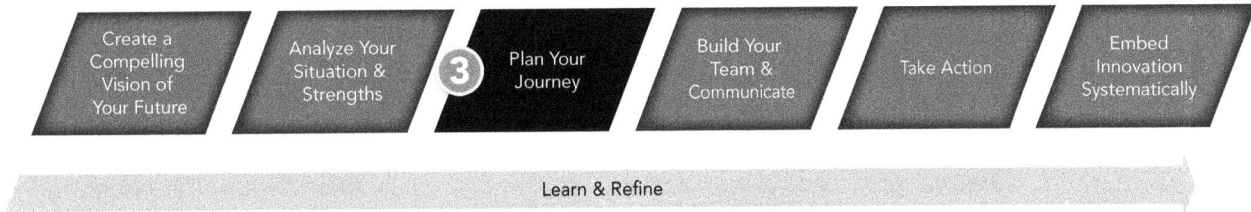

| Create a Compelling Vision of Your Future | Analyze Your Situation & Strengths | ③ Plan Your Journey | Build Your Team & Communicate | Take Action | Embed Innovation Systematically |

Learn & Refine

When you have a solid plan for your development journey, you begin investing your development time and energy based on your vision, your strengths and weaknesses, and your development goals. In order to stay motivated, it is important to experience a sense of measurable growth. Tangible results are especially crucial to implementing change, and demonstrating progress is a natural part of the expectation. An example is: If my boss wants me to show that I am a good leader before he will promote me, I need to show that I am "good" as measured by the boss's criteria. So, in this case, I would want to understand the criteria as well as know what the boss values, and build a plan that allows me to show those results. On the other hand, if I am developing for my own personal growth, I may not be as concerned about showing results to others, but will still want to feel I am making progress.

As you can imagine, some results will take longer than others to manifest. Our experience with clients has shown that leaders can certainly make quick progress in some areas, but other areas may take years.

Your life situation will also impact your development. For example, a leader may be a great provider for his family, and this is a core value he holds. He might create meaningful results that help cultivate developmental growth by focusing on specific behaviors that will promote his well-being and success. In other words through well-developed family relationships, he may simply experience a sense of progress ranging from a greater feeling of calm, clearer thinking, and better relationships with colleagues that will lead to better performance. He may also see measured results quantitatively using a 360° assessment (gaining feedback from several stakeholder groups at multiple levels within the organization including boss, peer, and subordinate) showing significant improvements in key leadership-related qualities. Another leader who wants to have a greater impact on the world may have an entirely different development focus and plan.

Consider the value of investing your energy in this journey as a way to foster meaningful change for the people closest to you. If you know, for example, that you have specific behaviors that are particularly difficult for your boss, an important colleague, or a loved one, you may want to prioritize those areas for improvement.

Options Development Plan Focus

To accomplish your vision, you may benefit from one or all of the following three developmental focuses:

- **Becoming more effective; developing new skills and/or behaviors** – Changing behaviors and building skills that will significantly impact performance, as measured by observed behavioral change, can create new opportunities. As you advance in your job responsibilities and/or as the organizational environment changes, you will continually need to build new skills. These can range from an understanding of how to leverage social media promoting your organization to building a board. In this category, the focus is on skills that can be developed through training programs.

- **Building on your current strengths** – Development can take the form of focusing on enhancing current strengths. It can also focus on important behaviors that adversely impact success. Again, we recommend focusing 80 percent of your effort toward building on your passions and the other 20 percent toward shoring up your deficiencies. This is a general recommendation; it is important to remember that your specific situation and needs will be clear indicators of what changes are required for your continued growth and success.

- **Minimizing your weaknesses** – In the SWOT analysis, you may have identified some behaviors that impede further growth. These may have been behaviors that made you successful in your current development (sometimes referred to as *overused strengths*). Even so, part of your development is examining the events and behaviors that got you here and understanding which interfere with your success as defined by your vision. For example, you may identify yourself as someone who is on top of every task. As your responsibilities grow, you will delegate more, but you may still feel uncomfortable with your lack of knowledge of the details. Trying to manage the details to the level that made you successful will become a weakness as you move up. It is important to tend to these behavioral changes as part of your plan. The challenge here may be shifting the focus away from daily details toward strategic thinking and expanding your ability beyond one or a few core strengths to develop several additional capabilities.

As you begin building your capacity, you may want to consider two distinct, yet essential, areas, external capacity and internal capacity. Though the research emphasizing the importance of both is compelling, most of our formal training still focuses on hard skills (external capabilities). This exclusive emphasis leaves many leaders ill-prepared for, and in some cases uninformed about, the importance of this internal capacity such as emotional intelligence and interpersonal skills. Research among Fortune 500 companies at Stanford University showed that 90 percent of those who failed as leaders did so because they lacked the interpersonal skills that are a critical component of emotional intelligence. This is confirmed by research conducted by the Center for Creative Leadership finding that poor interpersonal skills are a leading cause of derailment from executive-level positions. These terms are defined as:

- ◢ **External capacity (hard skills)** – Skills and behaviors associated with professional success. This is where most professional development efforts have been focused.

- ◢ **Internal capacity** – Includes intention, world view, purpose, vision, values, cultural norms, emotional stability, resilience, a sense of being grounded, overall personal well-being, intuition, balanced perspective, and attitude, and serves as the foundation for you to accomplish your deepest aspirations. Internal capacity is also required to move on to later stages of development.

In most organizations, the vast majority of development efforts focus on hard skills (including advanced degrees and certification programs), and thus, many leaders need to balance them by explicitly exercising internal capacity. To further describe this process, we use the term *mastery*, that simply means the capacity to not only produce results, but also to master the principles underlying those results. In other words, as a master, you can deliver results comfortably due to the internal capacity behind your skills and judgment.

Personal mastery involves enhancing your internal capacity to support the skills you have acquired while also removing barriers to your success. To help you achieve personal mastery, we recommend you enrich your ongoing development plan and personal practices (activities we repeat until we master them, like your golf swing).

There are some important factors to consider when creating your plan. First, you will get more leverage if you cross-train or develop several areas at the same time. According to Ken Wilber (*AQAL Framework DVD*), there are benefits to cross-training beyond simply focusing on one area. For example, people who both lift weights and meditate tend to make greater improvements in both areas than those who do only one or the other. Evidence suggests that a combination of activities from different parts of our lives complement one another. This is quite true in the leadership arena as well.

A comprehensive plan will take into consideration each of the dimensions that are foundational to human experience: physical, emotional, mental, and spiritual (people not comfortable with the term *spiritual* can substitute *altruistic* or *purpose*). If any of these elements are neglected, you are likely to find it will adversely impact your success in other areas over the long term.

There are standard programs designed to help this process. One of the programs we suggest is Integral Transformative Practice (ITP), developed by Michael Murphy and George Leonard. This practice involves a strong cross-training routine. Nine commitments form the essential building blocks of the ITP program. They create the roadmap for practitioners to follow to realize their potential through the cross-training of body, mind, heart, and soul. The commitments include aerobic exercise, mindful eating, strength training, staying emotionally current, a service component, and the ITP Kata, that is a 40-minute series involving movements derived from yoga and Aikido, deep relaxation techniques, imagery, affirmations, and meditation. ITP is a long-term program for realizing the potential of body (exercise), mind (reading, discussion), heart (staying emotionally current, community), and soul (meditation, affirmations). Joining a local ITP group can augment a strong individual practice.

Tools and Exercises

The range of tools is quite broad, so it is important to select something that feels safe and consistent with your values. The goal is to create a plan that you can follow and stick with to accomplish your goals. To help you get started, we put suggestions in Table 5.1. While several items fall within multiple categories, we attempted to classify them to be as mutually exclusive as possible. Some activities will provide benefits across several categories. An example of this is meditation, as it can help you manage your negative thinking, improve focus, balance emotions, and improve decision-making capacity.

Healthy development encompasses work in all areas. The practices you choose may evolve, and your practice may also fluctuate based on other life demands. We encourage you to maintain as much consistency as possible. Just as the benefit of exercise increases when you hit a specific frequency and duration, the same will be true for leadership development practices. The more you invest, the better your results will be.

TABLE 5.1: RECOMMENDATIONS FOR INTERNAL AND EXTERNAL CAPACITY BUILDING - ACTIVITIES TO CONSIDER INCORPORATING INTO PLAN

What activities can I do to impact my internal capacity (what I think and believe)?

- **Spirit**
  - Define vision
  - Define values
  - Pray
  - Participate in religious practices
  - Religious study
  - Seek spiritual counseling
  - Seek a spiritual teacher
  - Visualize goals
  - Become socially active – volunteer
- **Ethics**
  - Create guiding principles or values
  - Pay attention to ethics around you
  - Address situations you find unethical
  - Read and learn about ethics

- **Emotions (Emotional Quotient)**
  - Meditate
  - Seek therapy
  - Practice HeartMath™ techniques (the online resources and tools - end of chapter 5)
  - Practice shadow exercises - the ability to find in yourself the things you find frustrating in others and address them as growth opportunities
  - Keep a journal
  - Seek coaching
  - Maintain strong friendships

What activities can I do to impact my external capacity?

- **Body**
  - Exercise
  - Yoga
  - Relaxation
  - Weight lifting
  - Mindful eating/healthy diet
  - Sufficient sleep

- **Cross Training**
  - Integral Transformative Practice (yoga, Aikido, relaxation, visualization, meditation)
  - Reflection practices (do-reflect-learn)

- **Mind**
  - Read
  - Study
  - Attend lectures and discussion groups
  - Attend school
  - Perspective-taking exercises
  - Take stretch assignments
  - Volunteer for opportunities to build skills (charity work)
  - Manage polarities
  - Action inquiry
  - Mindfulness-based stress reduction

What activities can I do that impact us as a group (what we think/believe)?

- Review the list of activities, and determine which can be completed in a group; what groups do I participate in, and do they have similar values?
- Develop a mission and values as a family; you may choose to set family meditation time or gym time to promote a family sense of focus and well-being; many families share religious traditions and find that they provide a solid foundation and a shared set of values

What structures and/or groups will help? What groups or programs would support my development?

- Family activities could include how we eat, our exercise routines, our family reading time, our church or spiritual practice, and our volunteer activities
- Friend/social activities include what I do with my friends that support or hinder my development, such as exercise groups, emotional support, honest and accurate feedback, and dialogue practices
- Work events and support, including yoga classes, weight management support, fitness classes, insurance discounts for fitness, and smoking cessation programs
- Practice groups for development, such as Integral Transformative Practice, meditation, and church
- Study groups
- Formal education programs
- Informal education programs
- Fitness groups and programs, such as running clubs, ski clubs, exercise groups, and gym memberships

The following is a development plan template designed to help you create a plan that allows you achieve your goals. This table focuses mainly on identifying opportunities and the intentions behind your desire to change.

TABLE 5.2: SKILL/BEHAVIOR DEVELOPMENT WORKSHEET
Evaluate and Select Skill/Behavioral Change Priorities – Worksheet

Key Actions	Detailed Action Planning	Behavior 1
Select behaviors	Which behaviors do I want to improve or change? Which behaviors do I perform well that I would like to enhance?	
What are the consequences of this behavior?	What will happen if I continue to demonstrate this behavior in the future? How will my service recipients be impacted? How will my career be impacted? How will my colleagues be impacted? How will my organization be impacted?	
Why do I demonstrate this behavior?	I have developed behaviors over the course of my life because they make sense. What has changed to make this behavior ineffective now?	
How would I like to perform in the future?	Write an end-result statement describing the changes I will make and the impact of those changes. What will an observer see when I have made these changes?	
Who will help me change?	Who could I ask to provide me with feedback on how I am doing? Who could be a good mentor?	
What type of support do I want?	Make an agreement with a person you trust about how you would like to support one another in changing behaviors. How will that person hold me accountable for taking this step? How will I support them in changing their behavior? Is there a group that will support me in the long term?	
What will I do or not do?	What other actions could I take? What am I willing to commit to doing? What am I committed to stopping?	
When will I complete actions?	When will I have completed action items?	

The next template was designed to synthesize development activities reflected in the prior worksheets.

We recommend that all goals be SMART, a term referenced in the November 1981 issue of *Management Review* by George T. Doran. Smart goals comprise five characteristics:

- **Specific** - Goals should be definitive and clearly defined. When goals are specific, it is clear to see when they are reached. To make goals specific, they must clarify exactly what is expected, why is it important, who's involved, where is it going to happen. *Overall example of a goal: Teachers want to improve the reading levels of all the children in our program by 25 percent in one school year as evidenced by testing.*

- **Measurable** - Establish concrete criteria for measuring progress toward the attainment of each goal you set. Measureable defines what and how much change we are expecting. *Example: 25% in one school year is the measurement.*

- **Attainable** - When you identify goals that are most important to you, you begin to figure out ways you can make them come true. You develop the attitudes, abilities, skills, and financial capacity to reach them. You begin seeing previously overlooked opportunities to bring yourself closer to the achievement of your goals. "Attainable" ensures that our expectations are reasonable. *Example: One school year and 25% are reasonable goals; 80% in one semester is not an attainable goal.*

- **Realistic** - To be realistic, a goal must represent an objective toward which you are both *willing* and *able* to work. A goal can be both high and realistic. You are the only one who can decide the height of your goal, but be sure that every goal represents substantial progress. "Realistic" ensures we have the capacity to meet our goal. *Example: 25% is also realistic. Our children can improve that amount in a year.*

- **Timely** - A goal should be grounded within an approximate time frame. Goals lacking time frames also lack urgency. Being timely ensures we have a deadline to meet our goals. As Dan Heath and Chip Heath state in *Switch: How to Change Things When Change is Hard*: "Some is not a number. Soon is not a time." *Example: One school year is a defined period of time.*

Using the information from the worksheets and templates provided, you are now ready to complete your Development Planning Worksheet. This worksheet will serve as the foundation for the actions you will take to accomplish your goals, and should reflect your data gathering in the assessment chapter and your personal reflection.

TABLE 5.3: DEVELOPMENT PLANNING WORKSHEET
Development Planning Worksheet

Current State	Future State/Goal	Actions	By When?	Measure - How do you know?

David's Developmental Journey Continued

David will now walk through his worksheets and journal entries for planning his journey. When we last met David he had completed analyzing his situation and strengths. Now he is evaluating the impact of one of a couple of his behaviors together to determine how to best address them through his development plan. The output of this exercise becomes direct input to his development plan.

David's Skill/Behavior Development Worksheet

EVALUATE AND SELECT SKILL/BEHAVIORAL CHANGE PRIORITIES

Key Actions	Detailed Action Planning	Behavior
Select behaviors	Which behaviors do I want to improve or change? Which behaviors do I perform well that I would like to enhance?	(1) Time management (2) Technical oversight
What are the consequences of this behavior?	What will happen if I continue to demonstrate this behavior in the future? How will my service recipients be impacted? How will my career be impacted? How will my colleagues be impacted? How will my organization be impacted?	(1) Run the risk of burn out if time is not managed well. (2) Not keeping up with technical changes, since I no longer have direct technical responsibility, can make me less effective with both my internal and external customers and could negatively affect my company's reputation in the industry.
Why do I demonstrate this behavior?	I have developed behaviors over the course of my life because they make sense. What has changed to make this behavior ineffective now?	My technical ability is much of what has made me successful and opened the door to my current opportunity. Dramatic increase in management responsibilities makes for less time to keep current on technology and code changes.
How would I like to perform in the future?	Write an end-result statement describing the changes I will make and the impact of those changes. What will an observer see when I have made these changes?	Better time management will result in more responsibility being given to reports that will give me more time for high-level management and allow me to keep current on technology and, therefore, maintain industry expert status.
Who will help me change?	Who could I ask to provide me with feedback on how I am doing? Who could be a good mentor?	Both my direct supervisor and my key reports who have worked with me for many years and understand the industry and challenges. My supervisor could be a good mentor.
What type of support do I want?	Make an agreement with a person I trust about how I would like us to support one another in changing behaviors. How will that person hold me accountable for taking this step? How will I support them in changing their behavior? Is there a group that will support me in the long term?	I have a person that can track progress and keep me accountable for committed changes. This is a win-win-win for me, my associate, and our company—mutual support benefits all. The global teams have a very strong commitment to the industry and our goals and realize we all succeed or fail together so support will be strong.
What will I do or not do?	What other actions could I take? What am I willing to commit to doing? What am I committed to stopping?	Have in-person meeting with key stakeholders for input and buy-in and commit to supporting changes if the team agrees.
When will I complete actions?	When will I have completed action items?	I think this is a work in progress that will be ongoing but will have stages to measure progress.

Now we will move from the evaluation of David's behavior to creating the development plan where he determines what to do to address his behavior.

David's Development Plan

DEVELOPMENT PLANNING WORKSHEET

Current State	Future State/ Goal	Actions	By When?	Measure – How do you know?
Time management/ delegate better	Make clear objectives for additional responsibility for reports	Assign new responsibilities Set SMART goals for each segment of new responsibility	Year-end review	Document in formal review process Will be different for each area, but clear obtainable goals will be measurable
Technical Have been removed from technical— now depend on others for updates	Get more involved with lab in all regions for current technology as well as regional challenges or regulations	Commit to weekly meetings with technical manager to keep current	Start first of the month	Technical manager will evaluate my knowledge monthly at meetings via questions
Interdivisional communication is poor with different people chasing the same project from different perspectives resulting in wasted resources	Project status reports Monthly updates Clear channels for reporting	Create simple but effective document for tracking opportunities	90 days	Reports being filed timely
Lack patience with people not working to their potential	Improved understanding of employees' career goals Improved communication of expectations	Utilize relaxation techniques such as meditation and exercise Review behavior-based performance targets Take their value base into consideration when setting expectations so I better understand their true potential	Start immediately Have more personalized development plan by annual review including SMART goals	SMART goals will include project management criteria that can be tracked and scored. This will avoid misunderstood expectations

Innovative Leadership Reflection Questions

To help you develop your action plan, it is time to further clarify your direction using reflection questions. The questions for "What do I think/believe?" reflect your intentions. "What do I do?" questions reflect your actions. The questions "What do we believe?" reflect the culture of your organization (i.e., work, school, community), and "How do we do this?" questions reflect systems and processes for your organization. This exercise is an opportunity to practice Innovative Leadership by considering your vision for yourself and how it will play out in the context of your life. You will define your intentions, actions, culture, and systems in a systematic manner.

Table 5.4 contains an exhaustive list of questions to appeal to a broad range of readers. You will likely find that a few of these best fit your own personal situation. Focus on the questions that seem the most relevant. We recommend you answer *one to three* questions from each of the categories.

TABLE 5.4: QUESTIONS TO GUIDE THE LEADER AND ORGANIZATION

What do I think/believe?

- What are my priorities for development? Are they reflected in the plan I created?
- Am I willing to make the changes necessary to meet my goals?
- What do I consider personal short-term wins?
- Which wins do I want to see in what time frame? Is this reasonable?
- What do I consider a win for my team?
- What do I consider a win for the organization?
- Which short-term wins will be really important to key people in my life?
- How do I stay motivated to work toward goals that will take a long time, or a lifetime, to accomplish? How will I think about life changes, such as changing eating habits versus dieting?
- Have I taken into account the whole range of activities I need to create a sustainable change, such as involving others and creating a plan that I can live with long-term?

What do I do?

- How do I translate my vision into long- and short-term goals?
- Are my goals SMART?
- What are my financial goals and milestones?
- Is this a plan that is sustainable in the long-term? Will accomplishing my short-term wins motivate me to stay on track with my long-term plan?
- Does my plan contain the foundation work as well as skill building (i.e., basic health as well as business competencies)?
- Which wins can I identify and support that solve problems and are seeds for future shifts?
- Which changes in my behavior will demonstrate a strong statement to others and encourage their ongoing support, while possibly modeling changes that could also serve others?

> **What do we believe?**
>
> - Which wins will provide meaningful tangible and emotional results, and gain support of key stakeholders in my life?
>
> - Which wins will encourage others to engage in their own personal/professional growth initiatives?
>
> - Which stories can we tell others about the wins that were shared with the organization to encourage them to focus on their development?
>
> - Which wins are reinforced by our culture and values? Which wins would be opposed to our culture and values?
>
> **How do we do this?**
>
> - How do I align my goals and short-term wins with the organization such that I receive support for the changes I am making? How do I ensure that early wins are important to key stakeholders?
>
> - How do I track and measure my wins and their impact against overall personal and organizational goals? Do I have early warning measures?
>
> - Are my wins aligned with the larger organizational objectives?
>
> - Does the organization reinforce and reward the behavioral changes I am making?
>
> - How will I connect my personal wins to the organizational vision and measures to demonstrate the impact of my small steps forward?

David's Reflection Responses

We will now walk through David's answers to one or two questions from each section of Table 5.4. Simply follow along with David to answer the questions for yourself, or select the questions that fit your current situation.

What do I think/believe?

- *What do I consider personal short-term wins?*

  Time and resource management will be my first short-term win priority. In this hectic world we live in, we are always asked to do more with less, so we must adapt to manage with fewer resources. The first step I am taking is to prioritize what needs to be done since I understand it is not realistic to get everything done that is asked of me. This includes taking personal time to spend with family and friends, and enjoying hobbies and relaxation, perhaps, even taking an extra day on work trips to see local sites rather than heading straight to the airport as soon as meetings are done.

- *What do I consider a win for my team?*

  Obviously, from a corporate standpoint, financial results are very important, but we also must consider other things like efficiency, market share, and sustainability—from both an environmental and corporate perspective. If we have short-term financial success, it's good, but more importantly it indicates that we are growing the right way as individuals and as a team. If we are moving in the right direction as a team, I consider it a long-term win that gives us the momentum for the financial success we need to sustain and grow our business.

What do I do?

■ *Are my goals SMART?*

Yes, I believe my goals are smart as they fit all the criteria of Smart, Measurable, Attainable, Realistic and Timely. *Smart* because long-term time management and behavior modifications will benefit me personally as well as the team. *Measureable* in the time commitment for other activities as well as delegating responsibilities. *Attainable* because of the actions over which I have complete control that will allow me to make required changes as needed. *Realistic* as the changes I've committed myself to are within my control. *Timely* will be an ongoing process as business is fluid, and I will need to adapt as responsibilities and business demands change, but am committed to make the needed changes as demands change.

■ *Is this a plan that is sustainable in the long-term? Will accomplishing my short-term wins motivate me to stay on track with my long-term plan?*

I believe this is very sustainable as the team and I grow together, and we all will see benefits from the changes. Success breeds success; so short-term wins will give me and my team members confidence that will build momentum and reinforce commitment to the plan. I have seen this in the past few months where we have shown growth in market share and it has increased the team's enthusiasm to increase commitment and continue the trend. Some might worry about complacency with having achieved what we need to be considered successful, while we guard against this, I do not consider this a real concern.

What do we believe?

■ *Which wins will encourage others to engage in their own personal/professional growth initiatives?*

As I have stated before, I think team success will breed the desire for greater personal success. Fear of failure and pride in accomplishment are great motivators, and I think our experienced and motivated team understands that our personal and professional successes depend on each other and the team's success. Everyone—for personal pride and job security—wants to be recognized for their input and achievements, but I don't remember the last time I heard anyone say "I" or "me," it is always what "we" have or can accomplish together. New inexperienced team members might take some time to mature into understanding this, but if surrounded with good mentors, most will get to this point and those who do not may not belong on the team.

◼ *Which stories can we tell others about the wins that were shared with the organization to encourage them to focus on their development?*

Management personnel and goals change periodically in a large corporation; so we must always be aware we may be shooting at a moving target and must be adaptable to these changes. A few years ago, the management I started working for was greatly focused on high margins and being a full-service supplier in the agricultural chemical market. When this division was sold to another company, the new management had a very different philosophy with topline growth being the primary target under the assumption that if you sell enough, you spread the cost over enough volume and can be very competitive and, therefore, profitable. It turned out that sales and income dropped because the existing customer base was willing to pay for the service. Management was not interested in any service but cheap, and this strategy backfired. We lost business and money, and the company was sold again in less than three years. The third owner, after doing a financial analysis of the company, and seeing the benefit of the original owner's business plan, moved back to the original owner's philosophy and over time regained most of the business and income. Many good employees were lost in the transition, but some of the original core team was able to rebuild employee morale and regain the confidence of customers—but it took a great deal of effort by many. The take away from this is that even after losing good people and business, given the opportunity, the commitment and values of the people who had worked hard to retool the business plan were very successful. Developing yourself and your team will always pay dividends even if not seen immediately.

How do we do this?

◼ *Are my wins aligned with the larger organizational objectives?*

The organization has a set of goals and objectives as outlined by senior management that all plans cascade from top down to support the overall target. With this said, I believe the team's wins of profitable market share growth by adapting how we go to market and revising the product mix, anticipating market changes, needs and competitors strategies have served me, team members, my division, and the corporate objectives very well. If and when the corporate goals change, we will be prepared to refine our plan to adapt to the new targets, but I believe our core values and behavior will not need modification to stay on track.

◼ *Does the organization reinforce and reward the behavioral changes I am making?*

Yes, the organization is very supportive and has allowed me to add resources and change strategies on how we go to market during very difficult times when the market was at its lowest point in decades. Nearly my entire team is currently enrolled in an advanced degree program being fully reimbursed by the company that shows us they are committed to the team and its members. To be allowed to make dramatic changes at a difficult time and commit to the funding of the MBA program speaks volumes to me of the endorsement of the changes that have been and are being made.

Your Process of Creating Your Development Plan

Now that you have followed David's descriptions, it is time to complete the worksheets. Based on your assessment results, if you have not done so already, complete the SWOT analysis in Table 4.1 and *answer one to three questions* from each section in Table 4.2 for yourself. By internalizing your strengths, as well as opportunities, you can identify the gaps that, when filled, will help you accomplish your vision. Additionally, understanding your weaknesses will help you know what to avoid, what to improve, and what personal feedback to request from people skilled in those areas.

This chapter provided you with the tools and templates to create your development plan, and will help to close the gap between where you are today compared with your vision. The plan will greatly enhance your efforts toward actualizing where you want to be, as well as, making a positive impact on the world. Keep in mind that it is easy to create a plan that is too ambitious or complex. We encourage you to commit to small changes you can complete and then update your plan after you have accomplished your initial goals. The next chapter focuses on selecting the guiding team that will help you implement your plan.

Additional Resources

Books
Path of Least Resistance, Learning to Become the Creative Force in Your Own Life. Tool: Structural Tension. Robert Fritz.

Action Inquiry, The Secret of Timely and Transforming Leadership. Bill Torbert and Associates.

Crucial Conversations, Tools for Talking when Stakes are High. Patterson, Grenny, McMillan, Switzler.

Fifth Discipline Fieldbook, Strategies and Tools for Building a Learning Organization. Art Kleiner, Peter Senge, Richard Ross, Bryan Smith, Charlotte Roberts.

The Life We Were Given, A Long Term Program for Realizing Potential of Body, Mind, Heart and Soul. George Leonard and Michael Murphy.

Polarity Management: Identifying and Managing Unsolvable Problems. Barry Johnson

DVDs
Integral Life Practice Starter Kit. Integral Institute (3-2-1 shadow workshop and Big Mind).

CD Set
Mindfulness in Motion – A Daily Low Dose Mindfulness Practice. Maryanna Klatt, PhD

Online resources and tools
HeartMath™ meditation practices and emWave to monitor heart activity. www.heartmath.org.

Integral Transformative Practice. www.itp-international.org

What do I think/believe?

What do I do?

What do we believe?

How do we do this?

CHAPTER 6
Step 4: Build Your Team and Communicate

You are working on the fourth step in the process: Build Your Team & Communicate. The full process is shown below:

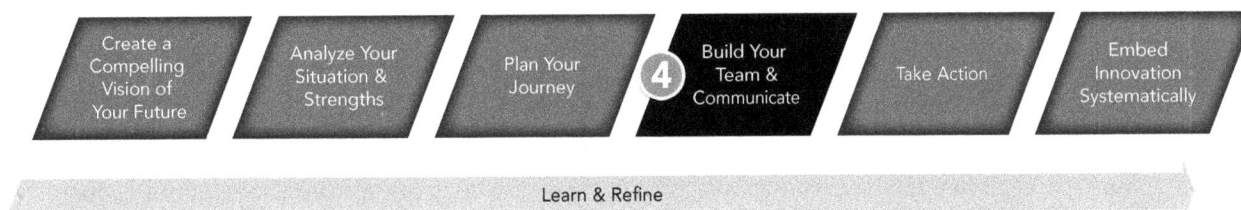

In this chapter, you will begin to identify the individuals you want to support your personal and professional development, and the specific roles you envision them playing during this transition. After selecting these people, you will consider the best ways to communicate your needs and receive their feedback. Here, you will carefully choose individuals you feel will be most supportive of your growth. Consider who is involved in your development and who is not. Your selection criteria should include: experience and skills in areas you want to develop, a high level of unconditional personal support, ability to offer constructive and valuable feedback, capacity to support your transformation, and ability to offer professional support and advocacy.

You will benefit from choosing a diverse yet trusted set of people to support your development. This is particularly beneficial if you plan to make changes that will significantly impact them as well. These people can come from various areas of your life, both personal and professional, and can have differing levels of involvement. Some, for example, could be fairly casual, such as a co-worker who is willing to give you feedback after a meeting about a specific behavior you may be experimenting with to meet a goal of improved interpersonal skills. At the other end of the spectrum, you could engage in a more methodical, long-term agreement with a formal mentor or coach. You will also want to consider the role your spouse or partner plays if you are in a relationship. Anyone involved must agree to give you honest and supportive feedback. The common thread for the people you ultimately invite to share in your journey is a firm trust and belief that, above all else, their support is unquestionably in the interest and service of your growth and success.

As another option, your development support could be found within a team setting. For example, if your goal is to run a marathon, your development support could come from a range of sources. It could be as simple as joining a running group to support a fitness goal. You might recruit very specific individual running partners. Other options could include finding expertise from third-party sources like running magazines or online groups that discuss tips and progress. You may even select a group with the explicit purpose to strongly hold each other more accountable.

Professional development can be supported in similar ways. You have a broad range of choices when looking for support. Organizations range from coaching and training firms to companies that help you improve your presentation skills. Depending on your needs, your individual selection of development support may have components of some or all of these choices. Some may be focused on hard skills, while others, like a coach, take on a more generally supportive role.

After you have selected your support team, the next step will be deciding on methods for each person to communicate authentic feedback. This is the stage in which you ask others for specific kinds of support, including possible behavioral changes on their part. You will be letting people around you know that you are engaged in a process of ambitious personal growth and that you want their feedback. Because people often create a sense of personal safety by being able to predict how others around them behave, it is important to inform the people closest to you that you are taking on a structured change process that may involve behaviors with which they are likely to be unfamiliar. The key message here should convey that this process will take time, and you will use these new behaviors with varying levels of effectiveness until you master them. You may say you are changing, and yet act inconsistently for some period of time while you master new skills.

While the information you share will change over time, the need for communication is critical throughout your development process. Communication will happen with different groups of people at various times, and will likely take on different tones depending on the audience and degree of impact. Some people will simply need to understand that overall change is underway, while you may want others to make significant contributions to support your behavioral change. What you communicate, and when, will depend on your relationship with the individual or group and the type of support you are asking for.

As mentioned earlier, during your process, you may also be asking others to change. For example, in the workplace, you may be communicating information beyond just the scope of work in order to help your staff, coworkers, associates, employees, and direct reports develop stronger business acumen. Moreover, you may want others to change their overall style of communication with you. As you model these new behaviors, be aware that some of your colleagues will adapt quite naturally, while others will require more specific and formal discussions to adjust to this new way of relating. As another example, you may want to delegate more and possibly different tasks, as well as give people more freedom to determine how they accomplish assigned tasks. In this case, you could open a dialogue explaining that you are trusting them to determine the most effective approach and will be available to offer support if additional input is needed. Though many employees would respond favorably to the openness, some will likely be confused if you are not explicit with what you are trying to accomplish.

Support Team Selection Criteria

Providing support to someone who is committed to a process of personal growth is an honor and a tremendous responsibility. It is important to select a support team judiciously since you are requesting these individuals be trusted advisors.

The following is a rough list of key selection factors as a starting point for you to consider when selecting your team. You may find other factors that are also important to you.

Performance: Consider selecting people who have mastered concepts, skills, or behaviors that you would like to develop in yourself. Performance could be as simple as that person having expertise in your field, or a field you want to explore. He or she could have strong interpersonal skills and empathy, or have hard skills such as financial analysis that you would like to enhance in yourself. These individuals could also be people you respect in general. If you are focused on developing advanced leadership skills, you could certainly benefit from the mentoring and support of someone you believe is successful against these measures.

Coaching: Consider having a person who is paid as an independent expert in the process of development and/or therapy. Most have undergone rigorous training or have significant experience in the field to support your development and success. As they are independent, they are generally free of the natural bias held by family members, friends, and colleagues. Working with the right coach can be very valuable, significantly accelerate the development process, and help you overcome barriers.

Therapy: Having someone who is an experienced psychotherapist can be very beneficial. A good therapist who is a good fit with your style and needs can help you make changes much more quickly and efficiently than if you try to work through issues yourself.

Personal or Family Connection: People from your family supporting your development could include siblings, a partner or a spouse, or a close friend who feels like family. Ideally, they will help you maintain a balanced perspective of your life as a whole, based on a historical connection, rather than just the immediate view of a new coach or therapist. They will also help you think through the impact of your changes on your family system. It is important to balance your development and professional focus with your family commitments.

Willingness and ability to commit time to your development: This is imperative. Ask those who are committed to supporting your development how to optimize your time together, and also discuss your mutual needs. The idea is that everyone should benefit from a clear understanding of how to both support the growth process and create healthy reciprocity. It will also be important to consider the time commitment you desire. Be willing to explore options that allow you to minimize the amount of time you request. You may consider creative options like volunteering for a board that your mentor or support person is on. This would allow you to learn directly and also support that person in meeting their objectives.

Consider not only who to select, but also who to avoid. Keep in mind that there are many very well-meaning people who would love to help, but, realistically, who are overcommitted and cannot provide the type of support you seek. Others may lack strong support skills, like the ability to give open and honest feedback. If someone lacks the time or skills to provide helpful advice, delivered in a supportive way, you should not include them. What you do not need during an intense development process is to waste time and energy with someone whose involvement could derail you.

Tools

The following worksheets are designed to help you connect your development action plan with the people who will help you accomplish these goals. They will fulfill different roles, ranging from encouragement and support to providing skilled expertise. You might also choose to include those who may be more directly impacted by the changes you are making. The more information you can provide during the process, the more likely they will be to support you or communicate their concerns to help you accomplish your goals. For an example, see David's answers following each worksheet.

TABLE 6.1: SUPPORT TEAM WORKSHEET
Support Team Worksheet

Goal	Type of Support I Need	Role	Skills/ Knowledge or Other Criteria	Arrangement

David's Worksheet

When we last connected with David, he had created his development plan. He is now evaluating who will help him implement his goals.

	SUPPORT TEAM WORKSHEET			
Goal	Type of Support I Need	Role	Skills/ Knowledge or Other Criteria	Arrangement
▰ Time management/ delegate better ▰ Make clear objectives for additional responsibility for reports	Direct reports	▰ Provide feedback on their ability to take on additional roles and tasks	Planning & time management	Monthly
▰ Maintain/improve technical skills ▰ Get more involved with lab in all regions for current technology as well as regional challenges or regulations	Colleagues in lab	▰ Provide technical information on regular basis	Chemist	Monthly
▰ Patience – improved understanding of employees' career goals ▰ Improved communication about expectations	Feedback from employees	▰ Guidelines ▰ Goals ▰ Reporting structure	Human resources	Quarterly
▰ Improve organizational skills through project status and reporting	Coach	▰ Evaluation tools ▰ Engagement techniques	Project management Organizational behavior	Bi-weekly

Once you determine your support team and their corresponding roles, you will want to figure out communication, timing, and expectations. This is the place to consider the kind of feedback you might expect from others to ensure you are making meaningful progress. This communication can provide you with invaluable information and feedback that is critical for your success. Since your plan is based on your own intuitive senses, the ongoing data should confirm your assumptions and serve as a feedback mechanism to refine your thinking.

TABLE 6.2: COMMUNICATION PLAN WORKSHEET
Communication Planning Worksheet

Who	What to Communicate	What They Can Expect From You	What You Want From Them	How Often

The following table is from David's Communication Worksheet. You can use it as an example of how one may use communication when managing change both personally and within an organization.

COMMUNICATION PLANNING WORKSHEET

Who	What to Communicate	What They Can Expect From You	What You Want From Them	How Often
Wife	How my personal growth is affecting our relationship Request input and involvement Serve as a sounding board	Lower stress level by delegating responsibilities Improved family time as I allow others' perspectives guide implementation of new roles Ongoing discussions	Listen Involvement Ideas Engagement Honest feedback	Daily
Coach & advisors	Clearly stated goals and objectives My reflections of journey	Better communication Clear targets with no longer "implied" plan Listen more, talk less Consider varying paradigm by region and allow this to be included in overall plan	Listen Advise Engagement & interaction Honest feedback	Weekly
Industry mentor	Short- and long-term goals Challenges Perceived obstacles	Questions Discussion of current and future issues Open dialogue with open mind to new and different approaches Paradigm shifts and how to adapt management style	Listen Advise Mentoring with learning skills Examples of how they have addressed issues successfully	As needed—monthly minimum
Direct reports	Delegate more – communicate tasks, due dates, and measures Discuss employee career goals	Regular discussions about expectations, targets, evaluation of performance and feedback Regular discussion of progress against goals (semi-annually)	Deliver feedback on regularly scheduled basis Direct and honest feedback Find opportunities for direct reports to take assignments to help meet their goals	What is frequency you would like (could vary) Semiannually, more often when appropriate
Colleagues in labs	New trends in technical fields	Questions & involvement	Updates on all formulation modifications Industry and regulatory rules changes	As available

Innovative Leadership Reflection Questions

To help you develop your action plan, it is time to further clarify your direction using reflection questions. The questions for "What do I think/believe?" reflect your intentions. "What do I do?" questions reflect your actions. The questions "What do we believe?" reflect the culture of your organization (i.e., work, school, community), and "How do we do this?" questions reflect systems and processes for your organization. This exercise is an opportunity to practice Innovative Leadership by considering your vision for yourself and how it will play out in the context of your life. You will define your intentions, actions, culture, and systems in a systematic manner.

Table 6.3 contains an exhaustive list of questions to appeal to a broad range of readers. A few will likely fit your own personal situation; focus on the ones that seem the most relevant. We recommend you *answer one to three questions* from each of the categories.

TABLE 6.3: QUESTIONS TO GUIDE THE LEADER AND ORGANIZATION

What do I think/believe?

- What qualities do I want in the people I ask to support my personal change?
- What qualities will I eliminate from my current and future team?
- How do I think my change will impact those close to me?
- Will my change help those close to me become more successful according to their definition of success?
- Why would others spend their time and energy to help me develop?
- How much support do I expect from others?
- Am I making reasonable requests of those close to me?
- Am I looking for others in the social service arenas who are making similar changes?
- Do I want people around me to change along with me?
- Do I need to improve my communication skills to improve my ability to seek support for my growth?
- Because my development may be a very personal and even private choice, what am I willing to communicate to others?
- How do I think my preference for privacy or sharing will impact others' responses to my changes and their ability to do what they need to do to eithers support me or accomplish their jobs? Do I solicit their input and support? If so, how and when?
- What personal stories (actions and emotions) will convey my commitment to my personal change in a heartfelt manner while also empowering others to act?
- Do I need to communicate anything to the organization or only to my support group?

What do I do?

- Who do I ask to participate in my change?

- How do I determine and communicate the criteria for the right people to support me ("right" includes personality traits, innate capabilities, skills, knowledge, time, and willingness)?

- Once I know the criteria, who are the right people, and how do I figure out what roles I would like them to take to support my success? How do I invite them to support this important personal transformation?

- Who do I need to support my development for it to be successful? How can my personal development activities or successes help these key people meet their personal objectives?

- Who may become a barrier to my change? How do I mitigate their negative impact? What are immediate steps and longer-term actions?

- What commitments and actions should I take that demonstrate my belief that change is possible?

- How do I "walk the talk" and show my conviction through my actions? Am I making the changes I say I will? Am I asking for input and acting on the recommendations others give me? If I do not take their recommendations, do I explain why?

- How do I ask for feedback? Am I clear about what information would be helpful to me and what information would not be helpful?

- How do I convey my request for input and support when I fall short of my stated goals at points along the way?

- How do I deliver messages tailored to different supporters that motivate them to continue to help me accomplish my goals?

- Can I be a role model for others during my change process to encourage them to expand their own capabilities?

- How do I convey messages that will make strong statements using the languages of both feelings and logic to appeal to each individual supporter?

- How do I demonstrate humility and genuine appreciation of the support others are providing?

- How do I communicate progress, new challenges and my commitment to what I am doing?

- How do I communicate the facts and my hopes for the future?

- How do I communicate that the balance between challenge and overload is important, and that I want to maintain balance as I move toward meeting my personal vision?

- How do I communicate my need and desire for accurate feedback?

- What do I communicate when my situation and priorities change?

What do we believe?

- What are the social and cultural norms that dictate the type of support I should ask for and expect?

- How do we use my personal change as an opportunity to test new behaviors and demonstrate their positive impact on the group (professional organization, family, community)?

- Do the current social and cultural norms still fit for where I am/we are going?

- Do I have the right support to change the culture of our group to allow me to sustain the changes I am trying to make?

- What are our beliefs about who does the communicating? How much information do they share? How often? Do we solicit input or just convey information?

- What is the appropriate language and message content based on the values, goals, language, and culture of each audience segment (organization, family, community)?

- What type of feedback will I seek from supporters to determine if they are supportive of my personal changes (this may be objective or subjective)?

- Does our current organizational culture and approach to communicating support me in making the changes I am trying to make?

How do we do this?

- What are the key skills and behaviors that support my transformation and are necessary to my team? What are the gaps between my current support team and the team needed to support transformation? Do I have the right people available with the right skills and behaviors? Do I need to augment my support team with professionals such as a coach, therapist, spiritual advisor, clergy, colleague, or boss?

- What is the best combination of approaches for me to meet my support needs? Does this include hiring a coach, or scheduling regular lunches with a trusted colleague?

- What trust-building activities can we conduct to improve my degree of comfort with those supporting me?

- What personal and professional metrics should I track to understand if I am seeking and receiving the appropriate level of support?

- If the transformation is a long one, how do I acknowledge the support others are providing? What happens if someone I thought would be a good supporter does not work out?

- Am I communicating what supporters believe is important to them? Do they see the progress they hope to see?

- How do I communicate wins to stakeholders to sustain their reinforcement and energy?

- What is my communication approach and plan? Who wants information? When? Through what medium? What are the key messages? How do I keep multiple supporters informed with the right amount of information at the right time to enhance buy-in and support for my behavioral change?

- Do we have any applicable stories connected with group folklore? ("Remember the time xxx did xxx? Guess what happened to me this week.")

- Can we combine and/or eliminate any current communications? Are we talking about things that are not supportive of the change I want to make?

- Would communication be more effective if my changes were discussed in conjunction with other topics that either impact or are impacted by my change (If, as a group, we are trying to change, maybe we can talk about our progress, or about personal and organizational changes and how they are linked and impact one another.)?

David's Response to Reflection Questions

We will now walk through David's answers to one or two questions from each section of Table 6.3. Simply follow along with David to answer the questions for yourself, or select the questions that fit your current situation.

What do I think/believe?

- *How do I think my change will impact those close to me?*

  I hope it will allow me to be a more engaged leader who listens more and tells less. The people I work closely with are very experienced and have had considerable opportunities to engage with me in many different situations. Because of this, they will benefit (as I do) in a more open and engaging style that gives them more autonomy and opportunity.

- *Why would others spend their time and energy to help me develop?*

  No one is an island, and I believe in my personal life, as well as my professional life, others around me will benefit from my growth and may very well grow themselves at the same time.

What do I do?

- *What commitments and actions should I take that demonstrate my belief that change is possible?*

  I must make my planned changes known to those working with me by setting SMART goals, then keeping people updated as I progress toward my goals. If my goals are not Measurable and Specific, they will not show my commitment and, therefore, make tracking progress difficult—not demonstrate my belief that the changes can and will be made. Timely reporting when these goals are attained will reinforce my commitment and progress. I also will utilize the feedback and input from my wife on personal improvements to dedicate personal and family time to improve balance in my life.

- *Can I be a role model for others during my change process to encourage them to expand their own capabilities?*

  Yes by closely working with colleagues and others, my changes will serve as encouragement that if I can make these changes so can they—and, if we work together, we'll all grow and improve. I believe everyone in my group feels strongly about improving themselves where they can, and think they will gladly support and join in any process for improvement. The more open dialogue is and the clearer the objectives are will also make others more engaged and excited to participate in our collective growth that will allow us to reap personal and professional rewards.

What do we believe?

- *Do I have the right support to change the culture of our group to allow me to sustain the changes I am trying to make?*

  I believe the answer is yes. We have made changes in the last few years and with this have seen progress and improvement in our business. This baseline success will serve me well in further changes, as success breeds success and confidence builds with it.

- *Do the current social and cultural norms still fit for where I am/we are going?*

  The norms are fluid and changing as we move more toward a global business environment every day. For example, during the writing of this, some of our corporate strategy changed and some regions of the world will remain independent. As a result, some responsibilities and reporting will change, but I do not view this as a negative thing. We just need to adapt and focus on areas where we have authority and responsibility. I have no control over change, but I do have control over how I react to the change. I've learned over the years that resistance is usually futile, so I believe we must adapt and grow with the changes. This being said, I believe, yes, the social and cultural norms do fit where my team and I are going.

How do we do this?

- *What is the best combination of approaches for me to meet my support needs? Does this include hiring a coach or scheduling regular lunches with a trusted colleague?*

  I have a trusted support group—most of whom are coworkers—that I think will support me well. We can communicate frequently as time and needs demand. I also have resources I plan to utilize from the university board on which I serve that will give a very different prospective. They have vast experiences from a different paradigm that will bring an excellent diversity and perspective to my support team. With them it will likely mean setting up monthly lunches or discussions away from the business environment.

- *What is my communication? Do we have any applicable stories connected with group folklore? ("Remember the time xxx did xxx? Guess what happened to me this week.")*

  With many years' experience in traveling around the world I have many stories that can support my direction and that of my team. I had one business associate that went into a different culture with the idea that the American way was the only way. He made it known that this Asian culture would need to adapt to his ways, as he had no intention of doing business their way. As you can imagine, this closed minded approach was not successful and he and our company were alienated from the locals. He arrogantly believed that when others come to our country they should learn English and adapt to our culture; however, when he went to their culture he expected them to adapt to him. Having traveled to the Middle East for a number of years, I was very careful to study their customs and traditions before going, and learned to show respect for theirs when in their country. Because of this, I have been very successful and am always invited and welcomed back.

Your Individual Process to Build Your Team and Communicate

Now that you have seen the worksheets and read through David's narratives, it is time to complete the worksheets and answer the questions for yourself. Based on your support preferences, complete Table 6.1 (Support Team worksheet) and Table 6.2 (Communication Planning worksheet), then *answer one to three questions* from each section in Table 6.3.

This chapter serves to help you clarify your supporters and communication plan as you begin defining your feedback sources. This is the plan that will provide you with expertise, emotional support, buy-in, and feedback for your development. While creating a communication plan may seem extraneous, never underestimate the value of both emotional/moral support and communication with those who will be affected by your changes. This could be as simple as talking to your spouse or family about the way changing your routine may impact them, while letting them know you appreciate their willingness to be flexible.

Resources

Books
Crucial Conversations, Tools for Talking when Stakes are High. Patterson, Grenny, McMillan, Switzler.

Fifth Discipline Fieldbook, Strategies and Tools for Building a Learning Organization. Art Kleiner, Peter Senge, Richard Ross, Bryan Smith, Charlotte Roberts. See section on Conversational Recipes.

The Fifth Discipline: Strategies and Tools for Building a Learning Organization. Senge, Kleiner, Roberts, Smith

What do I think/believe?

What do I do?

What do we believe?

How do we do this?

CHAPTER 7
Step 5: Take Action

You are working on the fifth step in the process: Take Action.

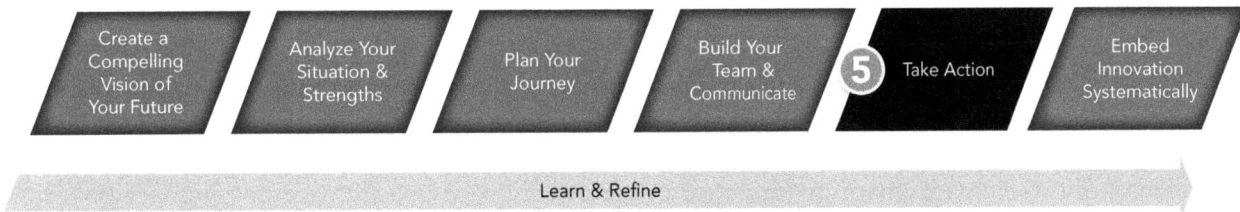

| Create a Compelling Vision of Your Future | Analyze Your Situation & Strengths | Plan Your Journey | Build Your Team & Communicate | ⑤ Take Action | Embed Innovation Systematically |

Learn & Refine

Now that you have created a plan to become an innovative leader and have defined your support team, it is time to take action. Your plan should spell out which actions you want to take, how often, and who can support your progress.

As you begin realizing your vision, you may start to identify challenges to your growth and development. Barriers are simply a normal part of any transformative process; we have provided a number of useful tools to help pinpoint and navigate them successfully.

An important part of your success is the belief that you can make progress and sustain growth in your leadership ability. You've already developed a strong foundation by creating a compelling vision and analyzing unique challenges and opportunities to determine what actions you needed to take to achieve your goals.

Be aware that this stage can take tremendous focus and energy. Many people stumble here, especially when the change process becomes difficult and the demands of balancing life requirements take on greater urgency. Think, for example, of how many times you may have joined a gym, but did not follow your plan to go there as frequently as you'd intended. Implementing your plan requires a deep commitment to your growth and also an understanding of the barriers you will face based on your personality type or history with implementing change. As barriers surface, you have the ability to remove them or modify your course with the support of your team.

With this in mind, allow yourself some flexibility in your development process instead of viewing your plan as fixed. See your plan as an initial starting point or a working hypothesis about how you will develop. With that perspective, you can better use the challenges you face as a way to provide feedback on your original hypothesis and modify it as you go along. In other words, rather than viewing these obstacles as threats, you have the opportunity to naturally incorporate them as fine-tuning mechanisms. For each challenge you face, carefully consider the unique learning opportunity and how to use it to help you implement your plan. Since personal development is a long-term journey, you will have many opportunities to face these challenges and take corrective actions.

Lastly, your support team will play a meaningful role in helping make the plan sustainable. They will offer you input and feedback as well as encouragement during times when you struggle. Even though you specifically chose the changes and goals within your plan, it is often still helpful to have a built-in system of accountability. When you run into inner resistance and difficulty, connect with someone who will remind you that you are already competent and that you can meet these goals in the same way you have met many other challenges.

Tools

The following worksheet helps you to anticipate barriers and mitigate them while implementing your action plan. You can refer to David's completed worksheets as an example.

TABLE 7.1: BARRIERS ACTION PLANNING WORKSHEET

Category	Barrier	Impact of Barrier	How to Remove or Work Around	Support I Need to Remove or Work Around
In my thinking				
In my behavior				
In our beliefs				
In how we do things				

David's Worksheet

When we last met David, he was building his support team and defining how he wanted to communicate.

BARRIER ACTION PLANNING WORKSHEET

Category	Barrier	Impact of Barrier	How to Remove or Work Around	Support I Need to Remove or Work Around
In my thinking	Old paradigms	The reluctance of others to embrace new thinking may delay my desired changes	Persistence and the support of my advisory team, including ongoing feedback	I have habits and default approaches that I need to pay attention to in order to change
In my behavior	Drifting back to old comfortable ways	Over time progress will slow and perhaps move backward	Seek advice on best alternative solution if first approach hits seemingly unmovable barrier, and ongoing feedback	New paradigm from support outside close internal group with personal stake and preset opinion Feedback and reinforcement from guiding team
In our beliefs	Since we have minimal turnover, we have vast experience and some who may be resistant to change Reluctance to embrace new thinking "that's not how we have done it" is the response I will hear; I'll need to show reasons for new direction	Experienced staff finding reasons not to change or undermine results of new paradigm	Continual reinforcement of new method and demonstrating successes Leaders visibly reinforce new thinking and paradigms	Support and backup from management when new way is questioned Leaders continually reinforce

Category	Barrier	Impact of Barrier	How to Remove or Work Around	Support I Need to Remove or Work Around
In how we do things	When operating in crisis mode as we sometimes do, it is easy to backslide to old ways Discomfort with building new skills when we are comfortable with our current approach	New methods and procedures being undermined and abandoned	Always walk the talk. When things are hectic and in a reaction mode, stop and take a breath and think problem through Provide time to practice new skills and reinforce new thinking	Management, technical, quality, sales, and production with buy-in and support Integrate the new changes into overall performance management systems; rewarding new behavior and the people who quickly adopt changes

Innovative Leadership Reflection Questions

To help you develop your action plan, it is time to further clarify your direction using reflection questions. The questions for "What do I think/believe?" reflect your intentions. "What do I do?" questions reflect your actions. The question "What do we believe?" reflects the culture of your organization (i.e., work, school, community), and "How do we do this?" question reflects systems and processes for your organization. This exercise is an opportunity to practice Innovative Leadership by considering your vision for yourself and how it will play out in the context of your life. You will define your intentions, actions, culture, and systems in a systematic manner.

Table 7.2 contains a thorough list of questions to appeal to a broad range of readers. You will likely find some that best fit your own personal situation; focus on those that seem the most relevant. We recommend you *answer one to three questions* from each of the categories.

TABLE 7.2: QUESTIONS TO GUIDE THE LEADER AND ORGANIZATION

What do I think/believe?

- In what ways do I need to change my perspective or skills to succeed?

- To become more effective, what do I need to change about how I see myself or the world?

- Including beliefs, what do I need to let go of to make these changes?

- What do I see as my individual role? How does this role allow me to fit in different organizations, including my family?

- How can I effectively grow and empower myself? How do I support my success as well as the success of the organization(s)?

- How can I benefit from my own personal growth and development?

What do I do?

- What feedback do I seek that will allow me to correct, redirect, or recalibrate my behavior and feel motivated to make necessary changes?

- How do I request clear and concise feedback that allows me to grow and supports the growth of others?

- How do I determine what I am ready to change within myself and what additional support I require for those changes I am resisting?

- What help am I willing to request? Am I investing appropriate time and/or money to support my growth? Is the commitment I am making to my personal change consistent with the results I expect to receive?

- What creative solutions can I find to increase my personal awareness? Do I track my performance against my goals using logs or reflection activities?

- How will I identify times when my behavior undermines my success?

- What will I do when I find my own behavior undermines my success?

- Can I treat my competing commitments as learning opportunities?

- How do I encourage "bad news" as well as good from my support team?

- Am I looking for opportunities to visibly demonstrate my progress as my development process unfolds?

- What am I doing to retain my support team as time goes on?

- How do I manage my transformation over the passage of time? How do I focus on living my current life while concurrently focusing sufficient time on my vision and goals?

What do we believe?

- How will my changes impact my ability to be successful, based on the organization's reward system, and given its values, goals, and culture?

- What are the stories within the organization about effective leadership? How do my personal changes position me going forward?

- What stories of the past do we need to stop telling because they no longer support our or my success?

- How can we connect prior leadership development successes to my current development effort? How can we use prior success to reinforce our ability to navigate current leadership changes?

- What parts of our past failures were attributed to leadership? Do my development changes appear positive to the organization's success, or are they threatening?

- Does our culture support the behavioral traits I am trying to develop?

> **How do we do this?**
>
> ▪ What processes do we have that may serve as barriers to developing in the way I would like? Am I in a position to change the systems to remove these barriers? If so, how involved and complex will those changes be? If I cannot remove the barriers, how will I navigate around them?
>
> ▪ Are my changes aligned with the organization's guiding principles? If not, how do I navigate the gaps between them?
>
> ▪ Do the organizational structure and governance approach support my personal development? If not, what options do I have to resolve barriers to my growth?
>
> • What early warning metrics can I use to track the impact my behavioral changes are having on others? What leading indicators will alert me before any significant issues arise?
>
> • How can I leverage current or generally accepted mastery frameworks to gain support of others and explain the changes I am trying to make?
>
> • How do my changes fit into the current organizational reward system? If there are misalignments, what will I do to navigate the barriers and challenges?
>
> • Have I clearly articulated the changes I want to make and asked for the support of those around me, while allowing them to maintain their success in a dynamic and changing environment?
>
> • What communication processes do we use to provide timely feedback? How will these impact me during my development? How will my development impact others?
>
> • What communication, if any, do I use for those who are not supporting my development?
>
> • What is the organization doing to measure, communicate, and fund the activities required for my development?

David's Response to Reflection Questions

We will now walk through David's answers to one or two questions from each section of Table 7.2. Simply follow along with David to answer the questions for yourself or select the questions that fit your current situation.

What do I think/believe?

▪ *In what ways do I need to change my perspective or skills to succeed?*

Years of experience can be a very valuable in dealing with daily business and personal challenges; however, the danger is becoming too comfortable with how I have handled these challenges without considering alternative approaches. Another perspective I must always guard against is the cultural bias from my education and experience in the U.S., as I deal with people from around the world.

▪ *Including beliefs, what do I need to let go of to make these changes?*

I need to stop and think through possible solutions to new situations or business emergencies, although my instinct is to react. My belief that technology and cultures may change while basic business principles remain constant around the globe may not be true as ethics and social norms are culturally ingrained and greatly impact on business dealings.

What do I do?

■ *How do I request clear and concise feedback that allows me to grow and supports the growth of others?*

I must start with the SMART goals and when setting measurable goals include stage gate points that clearly state the required feedback. This should allow me, my team, and those around me to stay on track with growth targets.

■ *How do I encourage "bad news" as well as good from my support team?*

Again, referring to SMART goals being realistic and timely, I ask for all feedback to be complete and factual. Whether news is good or bad, we must have all the facts and relevant information to make informed intelligent decisions. I also need to impress upon all involved that they will not be penalized for delivering "bad" news. We often learn more from dealing with bad news than good, so withholding "bad" news may be a great hindrance in progress. The best way I've encouraged this is my consistent behavior over the years when people around me have reported the full truth, without reframing to make it or them look better. This consistent behavior on my part when receiving the truth—regardless of being negative news—has already created an expectation of truth telling.

What do we believe?

■ *How will my changes impact my ability to be successful based on the organization's reward system, and given its values, goals, and culture?*

In a global organization, change is inevitable with managers from different cultures bringing with them different methods and beliefs from around the world. With these changes, the overriding message of personal and professional growth is very strongly and consistently supported, and I believe it will positively impact my ability to be successful. Within the reward system perhaps this may not come immediately, but, long-term, it will, as patience and persistence will pay off as growth and improvements are realized. Our organization has consistently demonstrated that those who commit to growth and development are rewarded.

■ *What stories of the past do we need to stop telling because they no longer support our or my success?*

While I understand people often look to the past to shape their views of the company, I believe we need to stop dwelling on the past and our leadership changes. Looking backward at the people and the decisions that were made is counterproductive to our growth and progress. Some people have moved on voluntarily, and we cannot change what was done in the past. We can only learn from it and take the appropriate course of action to implement changes. This includes what seemed like mistakes or poor performance from other departments or groups, but rather than rehashing mistakes of the past, we need to help facilitate changes that positively impact all. It is rare that when we tell these stories we actually have all of the facts. This limited knowledge can cause us to have inaccurate and faulty views of what really happens behind the scenes.

How do we do this?

- *Do the organizational structure and the governance approach support my personal development? If not, what options do I have to remove barriers to my growth?*

I believe that as long as a business case can be shown to support the changes needed for my personal growth, the organizational structure and governance will be very supportive of these changes. Should barriers exist, I must be willing to listen to the objections and address them with factual strategic plans to overcome concerns. Input from negative sources need to be seriously evaluated and addressed to overcome barriers and can be a reality check to help me solidify my plan. One great example of the organization being supportive is that we were approved for a tailored MBA program. We now have our first cohort enrolled in a new pilot, and we expect to expand that program based on our early results. While it took significant work on my part to get this approved, the organization has demonstrated that they are willing to invest financial resources in developing their leaders when they can see a strong business case.

- *What communication, if any, do I use for those who are not supporting my development?*

I think I must always reinforce the positive changes and highlight the success we have gained from my development. With these positive changes, in time others can see that our changes don't criticize them or their ways, but improvements that will positively impact everyone. I expect that eventually those who are skeptical will see that the changes we are making are working in the best interest of the company and our customers.

Your Process of Taking Action

Now that you have seen the worksheets and read through David's narratives, it is time to complete the worksheets and answer the questions. We encourage you to complete all of the exercises and *answer one to three questions* from each section in Table 7.2. This process serves to help you clarify what your barriers to success are, and how you will manage or remove them.

This chapter summarizes the basics for identifying barriers to your ability to successfully accomplish your goals as described in your plan. It also asks you to monitor the systems you put into place to measure your success and take corrective action. The next chapter will walk you through the process of ensuring that the changes you make are sustainable.

Resources

Books

Action Inquiry, The Secret of Timely and Transforming Leadership. Torbert and Associates.

DVD

Shadow Module 3-2-1 Process with Diane Hamilton. Integral Life Practice Series produced by Integral Institute.

What do I think/believe?

What do I do?

What do we believe?

How do we do this?

CHAPTER 8
Step 6: Embed Innovation Systematically

This is the sixth and final step in the process: Embed Innovation Systematically.

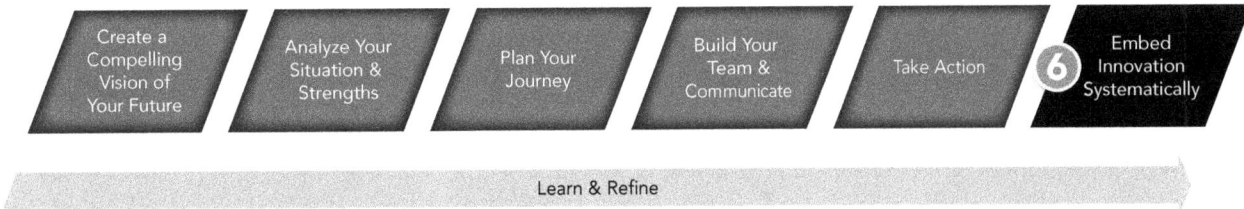

| Create a Compelling Vision of Your Future | Analyze Your Situation & Strengths | Plan Your Journey | Build Your Team & Communicate | Take Action | 6 Embed Innovation Systematically |

Learn & Refine

Congratulations! You have made it to the final chapter in your development process. You are now ready to shift from implementing your plan as something with a discrete end, to considering how you will integrate these changes into your lifestyle going forward. We suggest you view your leadership development as an ongoing process rather than something to check off the to-do list. Given the volume of change we now and expect to face in the future, continual development is a must—simply to stay current. In this light, you can begin asking yourself, "What supports can I put into place to stay on track? How can I gain additional benefits from ongoing practice?"

To maintain momentum, it is critical to retain a sense of urgency and minimize any complacency that may come from early success. Be aware that it is easy to stray from your goals if you declare success based on your early results, especially when other areas of your life tug at your time and attention. One helpful shift in thinking is to see the actions you are taking as a practice. You are practicing your leadership skills in the same fashion that a professional athlete practices a particular sport. The most successful athletes are constantly working to improve, even though they may already be the best in the world. This is why many of them remain successful over a long period of time. You will need to consider a long-term commitment to activities that foster success and help maintain your momentum.

So, ask yourself, "When I see progress, what will keep me motivated to continue practicing? I need some reminder that my progress is a result of engaged practice, and my performance is likely to suffer if I do not maintain proper focus."

By this point, you may want to re-evaluate your goals and begin raising the bar. You will need to balance long-term practice that sustains progress with identifying your next developmental focus or goals.

Altogether, this step invites you to be more conscious of actions as well as tangible barriers. Identify the elements in your life that support the continual realization of your goals. Also, examine the events and relationships that interfere with your vision and goals. It is critical to remove as many barriers as possible and to stop behaviors that no longer align with your development goals.

The overall objective in this chapter is to understand your habits and choices, and to confirm they are aligned with your long-term goals.

Tools

Below is a table you can use to capture and track your progress. For many people, the simple act of recording their progress in writing helps maintain their commitment. Use the following worksheet to help track your progress against each of your goals. If you would like to see a sample, review David's answers later in this chapter.

TABLE 8.1 PERSONAL TRANSFORMATION ACTIVITY/PRACTICE LOG TEMPLATE

Goal	Action	Record Actual Performance	Expected Impact	Priority	Measure	Progress	Feedback from Whom
Top 1	1.						
	2.						
	3.						
Top 2	4.						
	5.						
	6.						
Top 3	7.						
	8.						
	9.						

David's Worksheet

David will now walk us through his worksheets and journal entries for embedding change systematically.

PERSONAL TRANSFORMATION ACTIVITY

Goal	Action	Record Actual Performance	Expected Impact	Priority	Measure	Progress	Feedback From Whom
Top 1 Time management Delegate	Assign new responsibilities	Meeting conducted	Improved delegation	1	Document in formal review process	On track	Direct reports
	Set SMART goals for each segment of new responsibility	Goals established for all key people	Goal clarity	1	Will be different for each area but clear obtainable goals will be measurable	On track	Direct reports
Top 2 Build technical skills	Commit to weekly meetings with technical manager to keep current	Weekly meetings	Skills improving	2	Technical manager will evaluate my knowledge monthly at meetings via questions they develop	Slightly behind	Colleagues in lab
Top 3 Improve interdivisional communication	Create project status reports	Status reports	Clarity on activities and progress	1	Reports being filed timely	On track	Coach and employees
	Create monthly updates	Monthly updates	Clear understanding of inter-connections	2	Reports being filed timely	Slightly behind	Coach and employees
	Create clear channels for reporting	Develop communication plan and execute	The team understands what is required by whom and when	1	Reports being filed timely	On track	Coach and employees

Improved understanding of employees' career goals	Utilize relaxation techniques such as mediation and exercise	Meditate regularly 3x per week	Relaxation	2	Frequency	On track mostly	Self and wife
			Feeling healthier	1		On track mostly	
Improved communication of expectations		Exercise 3x per week for 40 minutes each					
	Review behavior based performance targets	Met with everyone on the team	Increased commitment from team	1	SMART goals will include project management criteria that can be tracked and scored. This will avoid misunderstood expectations that cause patience to be lost and feelings to be hurt.	On track mostly	Employees
	Take their value base into consideration when setting expectations so I understand their true potential better	Meetings allowed me to understand their values – I now consider them when possible and assign work accordingly	Increased commitment and professional growth of team members	2		On track	Employees

Innovative Leadership Reflection Questions

To help you develop your action plan, it is time to further clarify your direction using reflection questions. Questions for "What do I think/believe?" reflect your intentions. "What do I do?" questions reflect your actions. The questions "What do we believe?" reflect the culture of your organization (i.e., work, school, community), and "How do we do this?" questions reflect systems and processes for your organization. This exercise is an opportunity to practice Innovative Leadership by considering your vision for yourself and how it will play out in the context of your life. You will define your intentions, actions, culture, and systems in a systematic manner.

Table 8.2 contains an extensive list of questions to appeal to a broad range of readers. You will likely find a few of these questions fit your own personal situation; focus on the ones that seem most relevant. We recommend you *answer one to three questions* from each of the categories.

TABLE 8.2: QUESTIONS TO GUIDE THE LEADER AND ORGANIZATION

What do I think/ believe?

- How do I honor the progress I have made while maintaining focus on the balance of the work that needs to be done?
- How do I deal with both profound progress and a need for continued change?
- How do I deal with unresolved issues and uncertainty as I move forward?
- How do I deal with my desire to fix this issue and get back to the "real work?"
- What progress have I made as a leader/person?
- Are my assumptions still valid?
- As I have changed, am I still in the right role for my personal values and mission?
- How do I define myself as a leader? How do I think about my role and impact? How does my story about my effectiveness support or hinder my continued success?
- How does my belief about myself differ from how others see me?
- Am I still committed to the practices I developed?
- Am I willing to make these practices part of my life long term?

What do I do?

- What do I communicate that conveys both progress and continued urgency?
- Am I visibly doing what I have committed to doing?
- Am I living up to the standards I have set for myself?
- Am I perceived as acting with integrity with regard to meeting my commitments?
- What do I do that reinforces the impact of my personal development?
- What do I do to sustain my new practices and development?
- How am I continuing to show the new behaviors I have publicly and privately committed to?
- How do I continue to sustain the practices I have started and the behavioral changes I have made? Have these changes become part of who I am, or will I slowly slide back to old behaviors—especially under stress or as other priorities emerge?
- Do I surround myself with others who are focused on their personal changes so that I have a reinforcement system?
- Do I continue to track and measure my progress?

What do we believe?

- What do we believe about people who are always focused on their development?
- What do we believe about ongoing development practices versus fixing problems then moving on?
- What do we believe about how to monitor and build momentum in different areas of life?
- What do we believe about appropriate pace and focus on development and growth?
- How do our beliefs about growth impact our ability to maintain momentum?
- What recognition is appropriate from different groups in my life (family, work, etc.)?
- How do we see ourselves now? How has our image of ourselves changed based on my personal change?
- Will the organization's goals and values change based on my personal changes?

- How do we react to old behaviors that no longer support the organization?
- If our organizational stories about "who we are" change, do we incorporate new jargon, best practices, and human interest into emerging organizational stories?

How do we do this?

- What are the top three new behaviors others can expect to see? How will these behaviors be measured and reinforced?
- Who will remind me when I am struggling that I can make these changes?
- Do I clearly understand how my personal changes impact my work? Have I started to change the way I do my job? Have I informed others (discussed with others) how their jobs or tasks will change based on my changes? If my changes impact how we interact, have we agreed on the new way we will work together? Are we following a structured plan to perform consistently according to a new structure or guidelines?
- Do we need training to support new behaviors or interactions?
- What happens if I am not successful in meeting my top three goals? How would I like others to reinforce and/or support my behavioral changes?
- Do we have systems in place that discourage me from successfully accomplishing my top three goals?
- What processes/measures will we establish to identify behaviors that are no longer appropriate or necessary? What can I stop doing that will give me more time to practice?
- Are there any new ways to gain additional momentum to leverage existing changes and/or small wins?
- Am I reviewing measures regularly and recognizing results toward my change goals?
- Does the organization acknowledge leaders who have made the desired changes (job starts and stops) and mastered new skills? Am I being rewarded for my personal development in this system?
- Do we continue to measure and reward actions that are necessary to sustain the changes using the updated job descriptions and process metrics? Am I still a good fit within this system?
- Has the organization rewarded me with recognition, promotion, increased responsibilities, or financial rewards?
- Will others be expected to demonstrate behaviors and skills that I developed during my change? How will their changed behavior reinforce my new skills and behaviors?
- Have we sufficiently updated employee orientations and other human resources, and IT systems to support changes in goals and values for our leaders?
- Are we reviewing objective and subjective measures regularly and recognizing desired leadership behaviors for me and others?
- Are we reinforcing actions that positively influence the larger vision while inquiring into those that do not?
- Have we developed and tracked success?

David's Reflection Question Responses

We will now walk through David's answers to one or two questions from each section of Table 8.2. Simply follow along with David to answer the questions for yourself, or select the questions that fit your current situation.

What do I think/believe?

■ *How do I deal with my desire to fix this issue and get back to the "real work?"*

I have been using some relaxation techniques, including exercise. I have been biking 25 miles a week outside when weather permits, and a minimum of 40 minutes three times a week on a spinner bike when indoors. Exercising, along with reduced stress by delegating SMART goals, has allowed me to slow down and look more long term, rather than react, fix it, and move on.

■ *What progress have I made as a leader/person? Are my assumptions still valid?*

I believe I have made significant progress in behavior-based performance targets. With reviews, have asked team members for short and long term goals. I think my assumptions are still correct, and, with these changes, my team and I have a better understanding of where we, as a team, are heading—as well as each of us having a clearer career path to focus on. This is critical for each individual, as well as the team, as we look for growth and succession planning for our long term success.

What do I do?

■ *What do I communicate that conveys both progress and continued urgency?*

I will continue to do my best to communicate that, although short-term wins and/or gains are great, we must stay focused. Just as one good day does not make a successful month or year, we must feed off these successes and not relax and assume we have arrived because there is always someone behind us trying to emulate what we are doing—we must remain motivated to always being moving forward.

■ *What do I do to sustain my new practices and development? How am I continuing to show the new behaviors I have publicly and privately committed to?*

I have found that leading by example is still a very strong motivator. By following the new practices and sharing the results, even if not always as positive as you might like, you must be open and honest to foster trust and openness in others around you.

What do we believe?

■ *What do we believe about appropriate pace and focus on development and growth?*

I tend to be impatient with people and want results too quickly, but have worked hard to stop and think through the changes and what is required. This is a long-term journey and I must consider always moving forward after perhaps some quick wins. This may slow as the relatively easy issues are resolved and additional growth and progress may come slower and take more effort.

■ *What do we believe about ongoing development practices vs. fixing problems then moving on?*

I believe that the ongoing developmental practices goal is to greatly reduce the need to fix problems; consequently, the goal is to be more proactive in the development of practices and programs. Although you will never totally eliminate the need for crisis management, you will, over time, be able to reduce this to a manageable level. I believe we have made significant progress in this area, but will continue to adapt over the long term—that will have a significant positive impact on us, as well as our customers.

How do we do this?

■ *Are there any new ways to gain additional momentum to leverage existing changes and/or small wins?*

As we become better at controlling our own processes and become more proactive, we become more customer-focused and are seen as problem solvers and partners rather than just as vendors here to sell something and leave. With some small projects we won over the last few months, we worked hard to impress on the customers that we were there to partner with them and offer solutions, and have since been rewarded with several very large projects. I plan to continue to refine and develop this approach with training and programs to enhance and grow the attitude and skills needed.

■ *Am I reviewing measures regularly and recognizing results toward my change goals?*

This is a requirement with SMART goals and has continued to be very helpful to stay on track. Without these measurements, it would be easy to assume I am on target while not getting the full benefit of the intended changes. I will continue to track long term as this is a journey, and it would be easy to get sidetracked and backslide.

Your Individual Process to Embed Innovation Systematically

Now that you have seen the worksheets and read through David's narratives, it is time to complete the worksheets and answer the questions yourself. We encourage you to complete all of the exercises and *answer one to three questions* from each section in Table 8.2. This process serves to help you clarify what your barriers to success are and how you will manage or remove them.

In summary, this chapter helped you create an action plan and conduct thought experiments needed to sustain the changes you have invested so much time to generate. At this time in history, we culturally reinforce the idea of lifestyle changes like diet and exercise. This is also true of leadership development, awareness, and skill building. To sustain the changes you have made and continue to build on them, it is important for you to continually approach them with deliberation and a sense of presence.

In our dynamic environment, growth and development are required just to stay relevant. This is perhaps more true now than at any other time in history, where growth is now a requirement to achieve and maintain success. Leadership growth is not only a matter of conceptual and pragmatic learning, but being introspective about our relationship with ourselves and others.

Conclusion

Congratulations! If you started with the first step, you have finished the Innovative Leadership development process, and we trust you have seen a significant increase in your professional and personal effectiveness. It is time to celebrate your successes and the support you received from others! How will you acknowledge what you have accomplished? Consider reviewing your vision and SWOT analysis, and write down what you accomplished.

How will you acknowledge the support others provided? How, in your culture, do you show gratitude and appreciation? When will you celebrate with your support team, either individually or collectively? Have you already been celebrating?

What Is Next For You?

Through this workbook, we provided a framework for developing Innovative Leadership to support your success. We augmented the process with a series of reflection questions and templates that can serve as guides. Based on our work with several hundred clients, we offer this specific combination of tools and framework to create a comprehensive approach that will allow you, the leader, to define what you want to change and give you a road map to support your development.

We also provided the story of David to illustrate how to use the development process from a global perspective. He uses the tools in the book and answers the questions to illustrate how a highly effective leader would engage in development. It is through David's explorations that we share the practical application of this theory with you.

Now that you have completed the workbook and established a solid personal development practice, it is time to think about whether you want to enhance your practice and begin the process again. Do you want to build on what you have created and revisit parts of the workbook that may be valuable at this time? You could start from the beginning and confirm your vision and values. Future iterations will likely take less time, as you now have experience with the development process. You may find that you focus in different areas based on your growth.

Congratulations on the progress you have made on your journey toward Innovative Leadership.

Enjoy your success!

What do I think/believe?

What do I do?

What do we believe?

How do we do this?

How will you and your support team celebrate your success?

Appendix

By Melissa Stone, Ph.D.

This workbook, its exercises, and recommended considerations focus mainly on the fourth and fifth stages in Maslow's hierarchy of needs model. These stages address esteem and self-actualization. In many cases, when the leader is working in the context of a domestically owned global company, or in a large multi-national organization with operations in locations where democratic governance and rule of law provide for basic human security and access to quality public services of reasonable quality, the global leader and staff members will take responsibility for their own basic needs. They will address their own first, second, and third levels of needs on Maslow's hierarchy, namely the physiological, safety, love/belonging levels. Apart from a focus on resilience, helping the leader meet these needs is outside of the scope of this workbook.

However, in our increasingly global community, new business opportunities are growing at a rapid rate in countries where economic conditions, political instability, or a legacy of conflict create conditions where large proportions of in-country populations still experience significant obstacles to securing their needs on Maslow's first three levels. In these locations, global leaders and their colleagues are more likely to experience these first three levels of needs themselves in connection with their own working conditions and family situation; in addition, global leaders may be called upon to manage a broader range of human needs within the context of global business operations.

In such cases, the leader and the organization may face the added challenge and expense of addressing these issues. The leader may need to retain qualified international staff and costs may include additional benefits such as, but not limited to, long-term in-country accommodations and meals; additional security provisions; language and other training; emergency medical evacuation and supplementary life and healthcare insurance policies; annual or bi-annual home leave; as well as added costs for family relocation and education costs for dependent children. While the physiological, security and love/belonging levels appear to be at a lower tier than those of the esteem and self-actualization levels, they are significant in that leaving any one of these key issues unaddressed can severely compromise staff productivity—which directly correlates to business competitiveness, profitability, and overall sustainability.

Especially in startup businesses, cases in which companies merge, when the global leader is new to the post or has been recently transferred from another location, leaders may find that the time and effort required to manage the logistics and added responsibilities for ensuring their own and their staff members health, security, and well-being in more complex, less predictable environments is comparable to having a second job. In addition to having the obvious impact on staff morale and staff retention, the global leader's performance in this second job can include elements of serious legal liability, as well as long-term financial ramifications in cases where staff are injured, or worse, in the performance of their duties.

Corresponding with Maslow's first three levels of need, the following table includes recommended considerations for leaders and their staff that may be useful to leaders who are new to the global environment or are working in less developed countries.

Human Need	Recommended Considerations
1. Physiological Clean air Untainted/high quality food Potable water Medical care Sanitation	■ In cities with low quality air index, consider indoor climate control systems to secure indoor air quality in homes, in the office, and in vehicles ■ In locations where food inspection standards are undefined or irregularly enforced, or for staff with special dietary needs, provide access to quality food ■ Provide for reliable and tested access to potable water, as well as water for showering and household use ■ Plan for regular in-person contact with spouses, partners, and other families if overseas posting requires separation of families ■ Ensure that you and your staff have access to international healthcare services, supplementary life and disability insurance, and an emergency evacuation plan ■ Consider available hygiene standards to ensure that you and your staff can avoid exposure to pathogens associated with basic sanitation
2. Safety Includes security of: Body Home Property Employment Resources Social order Morality The family	■ Ensure that you and your staff have safe and secure premises for working, living, and the education of dependent children ■ Provide for safe transport, including vehicle safety assessment and maintenance ■ Consider provisions for ensuring job security and protection of personal and business physical resources ■ Maintain awareness that you and you company comply with the rules of the larger social order and culture, including local belief and family systems ■ Consider ways that your business can show support of the local community
3. Love/Belonging Friendship Community Family	■ Be supportive of your staff needs for friendship, emotional support, and community beyond the workplace environment ■ Consider work/life balance regarding family and need for intimacy and regular communications characteristic of healthy adult relationships, in addition to employee benefits that encourage reunions with or co-location of family members

It is important for global leaders to be aware of the potential challenges they may face when leading a global operation and also when taking assignments abroad. These challenges may be very personal and can take a significant toll on you as a leader as well as on your family.

References

Black, J. Stewart., Allen J. Morrison, and Hal B.Gregersen. *Global explorers: The next generation of leaders.* New York: Routledge, 1999.

Brown, Barrett. "Conscious Leadership for Sustainability: How Leaders with Late-Stage Action Logic Design and Engage in Sustainability Initiatives." Ph.D. diss., Fielding Graduate University, 2011.

Bueno, Cristina Moro, and Stewart L. Tubbs. Identifying global leadership competencies: An exploratory study. [Empirical study to investigate Global Leadership Competencies Model by Chin, Gu and Tubbs (2001)]. *Journal of American Academy of Business, Cambridge* 5(1/2): 80 (2004).

Collins, Jim. Good to Great: *Why some Companies Make the Leap ... and Others Don't.* New York: HarperCollins Publishers, Inc., 2001.

Conner, Jill, and Michael J. Marquardt. "Developing leaders for a global consumer products company." *Advances in Developing Human Resources* 1 (4): 22-37 (1999).

Cook-Greuter, Susanne. "A Detailed Description of Nine Action Logics in the Leadership Development Framework Adapted from Leadership Development Theory," www.cook-greuter.com. 2002.

Csikszentihaly, Mihaly. *Flow: The Psychology of Optimal Experience.* New York: Harper Perennial, 1990.

Dalton, Maxine, Chris Ernst, Jennifer Deal, and Jean Leslie. *Success for the new global manager: How to work across distances, countries, and cultures.* San Francisco: Jossey-Bass. 2002.

Fiedler, F. E.. Leadership experience and leader performance—Another hypothesis shot to hell. *Organizational Behavior and Human Performance* 5 (1): 1-14 (1970).

Fitch, Geoff, Venita Ramirez, and Terri O'Fallon. "Enacting Containers for Integral Transformative Development." Presentation: Integral Theory Conference, July 2010.

Friedman, Thomas L. *The world is flat: A brief history of the twenty-first century.* New York: Farrar, Straus and Giroux. 2005.

Gauthier, Alain. "Developing Generative Change Leaders Across Sectors: An Exploration of Integral Approaches," *Integral Leadership Review,* June 2008.

Goleman, Daniel. *Emotional Intelligence.* New York: Bantam Books, 1995.

Goleman, Daniel. *Working with Emotional Intelligence.* New York: Bantam Books, 1998.

Goleman, Daniel, Richard E. Boyatzis, and Annie McKee. *Primal Leadership: Learning to Lead with Emotional Intelligence.* Boston: Harvard Business School Press, 2002.

Hofstede, Geert. "Culture's Consequences: International Differences in Work-Related Values." *Sage Publications.* 1980.

Howe-Murphy, Roxanne. *Deep Coaching: Using the Enneagram as a Catalyst for Profound Change.* El Granada: Enneagram Press, 2007.

Kets De Vries, Manfred. F. R., and Christine Mead. The development of the global leader within the multinational corporation. In V. Pucik, N. M. Tichy & C. K. Barnett (Eds.), *Globalizing management. Creating and leading the competitive organization* (pp. 187-205). New York: Wiley & Sons. 1992.

Klatt, Maryanna, Janet Buckworth, and William B. Malarkey. "Effects of Low-Dose Mindfulness-Based Stress Reduction (MBSR-ld) on Working Adults." *Health Education and Behavior* 36 (3): 601-614 (2009).

Lobel, S. A. "Global leadership competencies: Managing to a different drumbeat." *Human Resource Management,* 29 (1): 39-47 (1990).

Maddi, Salvatore R. and Deborah M. Khoshaba. *Resilience at Work: How to Succeed No Matter What Life Throws at You.* New York: AMACOM Books, 2005.

Marquardt, Michael J., and Nancy O. Berger. *Global leaders for the 21st century.* Albany, NY: State University of New York Press. 2000.

Marquardt, Michael J., and Nancy O. Berger. "The future: Globalization and new roles for HRD." *Advances in Developing Human Resources* 5 (3): 283-295 (2003).

McCall, Morgan W., Jr., and George P. Hollenbeck. *The Lessons of International Experience: Developing global executives.* Boston: Harvard Business School Press, 2002.

Mendenhall, Mark E., Joyce Osland, Allan Bird, Gary R. Oddou, and Martha L. Maznevski. *Global leadership: Research, practice and development*. New York: Routledge. 2008.

Metcalf, Maureen. "Level 5 Leadership: Leadership that Transforms Organizations and Creates Sustainable Results." *Integral Leadership Review*. March 2008.

Metcalf, Maureen, John Forman, and Dena Paluck. "Implementing Sustainable Transformation – Theory and Application." *Integral Leadership Review*. June 2008.

Moran, Robert. T., and John R. Riesenberger, *The global challenge: Building the new worldwide enterprise*. London: McGraw-Hill. 1994.

Northouse, Peter G. *Leadership: Theory and Practice*. Thousand Oaks: Sage Publications, 2010.

O'Fallon, Terri, Venita Ramirez, Jesse McKay, and Kari Mays. "Collective Individualism: Experiments in Second Tier Community." Presented August, 2008 at the Integral Theory Conference.

O'Fallon, Terri. "The Collapse of the Wilber-Combs Matrix: The Interpenetration of the State and Structure Stages." Presented July, 2010 at the Integral Theory Conference (1st place winner).

O'Fallon, Terri. "Integral Leadership Development: Overview of our Leadership Development Approach." www.pacificintegral.com, 2011.

Patterson, Kerry, Joseph Grenny, Ron McMillan, and Al Switzler. *Crucial Conversations: Tools for talking when stakes are high*. New York: McGraw-Hill, 2002.

Rhinesmith, Stephen H. *A manager's guide to globalization: Six skills for success in a changing world* (Second ed.). New York: McGraw-Hill. 1996.

Richmer, Hilke R. An Analysis of the Effects of Enneagram-Based Leader Development on Self-Awareness: A Case Study at a Midwest Utility Company. Ph.D. diss., Spalding University, 2011.

Riso, Don Richard, and Russ Hudson. *The Wisdom of the Enneagram: The Complete Guide to Psychological and Spiritual Growth for the Nine Personality Types*. New York: Bantam, 1999.

Riso, Don Richard and Russ Hudson. *Personality Types: Using the Enneagram for Self-Discovery*. New York: Houghton Mifflin, 1996.

Rooke, David and William R. Torbert. "Seven Transformations of Leadership, Leaders are made, not born, and how they develop is critical for organizational change," *Harvard Business Review*, April 2005.

Rooke, David and William R. Torbert. "Organizational Transformation as a Function of CEOs' Developmental Stage." *Organization Development Journal* 16 (1): 11-28 (1998).

Rosen, Robert, Patricia Digh, Marshall Singer, and Carl Phillips. *Global Literacies: Lessons on business leadership and national cultures*. New York: Simon & Schuster. 2000.

Torbert, William R. and Associates. *Action Inquiry – The Secret of Timely and Transforming Leadership*. San Francisco: Berrett-Koehler Publishing, Inc. 2004.

Senge, Peter, Art Kleiner, Charlotte Roberts, Richard Ross, and Bryan Smith. *The Fifth Discipline Fieldbook: Strategies and Tools for Building a Learning Organization*. New York: Doubleday, 1994.

Spreitzer, Gretchen M., Morgan W. McCall, Jr., and Joan D. Mahoney. "Early identification of international executive potential." *Journal of Applied Psychology* 82 (1): 6-29 (1997).

Terrell, Steve. Learn From Experience. *Leadership Excellence*, June 2013.

Terrell, Steve. Learning Mindset: Developing Leaders through Experience. trainingmag.com. March 2014.

Terrell, Steve, and Katherine, Rosenbusch. "How global leaders develop," *Journal of Management Development* 32 (10): 1056-1079 (2013).

Wigglesworth, Cindy. "Why Spiritual Intelligence Is Essential to Mature Leadership," *Integral Leadership Review*, August, 2006.

Wilber, Ken. "Introduction to Integral Theory and Practice: IOS Basic and AQAL Map." www.integralnaked.org. 2003.

Author Bio

Maureen Metcalf

Maureen is the founder and CEO of Metcalf & Associates, Inc., a management consulting and coaching firm dedicated to helping leaders, their management teams, and organizations implement the Innovative Leadership practices necessary to thrive in a rapidly changing environment.

Maureen is an acclaimed thought leader who developed, tested, and implemented emerging models that dramatically improve leaders and organization's success in changing times. She works with leaders to develop Innovative Leadership capacity and with organizations to further develop Innovative Leadership qualities. Maureen is at the forefront of helping organizations to explore these emerging solutions for long-term organizational sustainability.

As a senior manager with two "Big Four" management consulting firms for 12 years, Maureen managed and contributed to successful completion of a wide array of projects from strategy development and organizational design for start-up companies to large system change for well-established organizations. She has worked with a number of Fortune 100 clients delivering a wide range of significant business results such as: increased profitability, cycle time reduction, increased employee engagement and effectiveness, and improved quality.

Author Bio

Steve Terrell

Steve Terrell, president and founder of Aspire Consulting, is a leadership development consultant with 30 years of experience in improving organizational and human performance. Through his varied experiences, he has developed deep and broad capabilities in a wide range of executive/leadership development approaches, in a variety of organizations, as both an internal and external consultant.

Steve works with clients to build leadership capabilities; design, develop, and implement management/leadership curricula; and advise executive/leadership development professionals on the development of leadership development strategy, curriculum, and programs. He is a trusted practitioner with deep knowledge of global leadership development, having earned his doctorate studying how global leaders develop.

Steve's career has progressed through the Virginia Department of Corrections, Bank of America, Andersen Consulting, Dove Consulting, and Executive Development Associates. He founded Aspire Consulting in 2002 with the mission of helping organizations turn their vision into reality. His work has taken him throughout the United States, and to the United Kingdom, Germany, France, Australia, and Singapore.

Steve received his B.A. in Music Composition and his M.S. Ed. in Education (Counseling) from Old Dominion University, and his doctorate in Human Resource Development from The George Washington University. He is an adjunct faculty member at Old Dominion University.

Author Bio

Ben Mitchell

Ben manages the fenestration coatings business for residential and commercial building products including R & D, sales, and marketing for the Americas as well as oversight for the Middle East and Asia Pacific markets. A member of the American Institute of Architects and the Construction Specification Institute, he serves as chair, Finishing Task Group for Aluminum Materials, for the American Architectural Manufacturers Association.

He first joined Akzo Nobel Coatings, Inc., in 1990 as a lab technician and was then promoted to a senior chemist where he formulated high-performance coatings for the fenestration industry before he assumed the position of Global Technical Service Manager, Extrusion Coatings in 1997.

Ben also serves on the Board of Trustees for Urbana University in Urbana, Ohio, where he serves on the Executive Committee. He was instrumental in the 2013 strategic planning and board restructuring process.

A member of the American Institute of Architects and the Construction Specification Institute, Ben served on the technical committee of the National Fenestration Ratings Council. He serves as chair, Finishing Task Group for Aluminum Materials, for the American Architectural Manufacturers Association. In this role, he guides the committee in writing coating specifications for window and curtain wall and commercial construction industries. He also serves on the technical committee for the Window and Door Manufacturer Association and is a member of the Glass Association of North America. As a delegate for the Council on Tall Buildings and Urban Habitat, he attends their global seminars and meetings.

When he is not traveling, he enjoys being home in Glenford, Ohio, southeast of Columbus, with his wife, Paula. They have three grown children and six grandchildren ranging in age from 4 months to 6 years. They also own a Christmas tree farm with over 3,000 trees that will be the right size to start selling in the next couple of years.

During his lifetime, he has moved twenty-six times and has flown over two million miles.

Thank you for reading!

Thank you for taking the time to read the *Innovative Leadership Workbook for Global Leaders.*

I trust the worksheets and reflection questions you completed here will help you become a more effective leader. Because growth has a ripple-effect dynamic, we welcome your suggestions, additional tools, and templates. Please contact me at:

> Maureen Metcalf
> Metcalf & Associates, Inc.
> MMetcalf@metcalf-associates.com

This is the fourth in a series of workbooks. Download other titles on Innovative Leadership at www.innovativeleadershipfieldbook.com.